Cooking *in the* Lowcountry

FROM

THE OLD POST OFFICE

≋ | RESTAURANT | ≋

Cooking in the Lowcountry

FROM

THE OLD POST OFFICE

≋| RESTAURANT |≋

JANE & MICHAEL STERN

RUTLEDGE HILL PRESS®
A Division of Thomas Nelson Publishers
Since 1798

www.thomasnelson.com

Published by Rutledge Hill Press, a Division of Thomas Nelson, Inc.,
P.O. Box 141000, Nashville, Tennessee, 37214.

Library of Congress Cataloging-in-Publication Data

Stern, Jane.
    The lowcountry cookbook from the Old Post Office restaurant / Jane & Michael Stern.
      p. cm.
    Includes index.
    ISBN 1-4016-0146-4 (hardcover)
    1. Cookery, American—Southern style. 2. Cookery—SouthCarolina—Charleston. 3. Old Post Office (Restaurant)
I. Stern, Michael, 1946– II. Title.
TX715.2.S68S83 2004
641.59757—dc22   2004004376

Printed in the United States of America

04 05 06 07 08—5 4 3 2

Contents

Foreword

In the mid 1980s, I began my dream to open a restaurant on beautiful Edisto Island. Because the island was still very much "undiscovered" by tourists then and the location was well up the road from the beach, I was given little chance of ever making it.

Thank goodness two people bothered to listen to me and only three believed in me: my late father J. R. Bardin, my partner David Gressette, and myself. With a little seed money from Pops J and a lot of begging, clawing, and scratching for money by my loyal partner, we finally—nearly three years later—opened The Old Post Office in May of 1988. Right before opening day the number of people convinced we would make it had dwindled to two: David and me.

Now as we begin our seventeenth year, what started as a dream has become a restored landmark where generations come to meet time and time again—just like they did when the premises housed the U.S. Post Office. *Employee* is a word seldom used as The Old Post Office staff is more of a family. Our manager, Peter Sanders, has been with us since day one, and Ruthie Paulsen Bell, who heads our wait staff, has been charming and humoring guests since 1990. Most of the others have been with us at least four or five years. There is an old saying on Edisto, "Someone has to die to get a job waiting tables at The Old Post Office."

In the back of the house we have made dishwashing a respectable position with many graduating to become chefs, engineers, and one doctor that I know of. There are no uniforms and we deploy an informal freehand approach that would drive all other restaurateurs mad. I am grateful first and foremost to my staff and to our wonderful customers. I thank my lucky stars for the great fortune we have gotten from the press and particularly glad that two heroes of mine, Jane and Michael Stern, happened to come in here one night.

Within these pages are many of our most beloved recipes. I welcome you to feel free to go strictly by the book or do as we do at The Old Post Office and work with an imaginative free hand and unstructured pursuit of pleasure.

—Philip Bardin

Acknowledgments

What a joy it was to spend time on Edisto Island with Philip Bardin. A great host and masterful chef, a true horse lover and a good friend, he made working on this book nothing but a pleasure for us. We thank him for putting so much of himself into this project as he has into his restaurant.

Our comrades at Rutledge Hill Press have made a reality of our dream of commemorating favorite restaurants around the country in a series of Roadfood cookbooks. In particular, we thank Roger Waynick and Larry Stone, who share our passion for great meals around the country, and whose support and belief in this series make it happen. We also thank Geoff Stone for his scrupulous editing and Bryan Curtis for his good ideas to spread the word.

We are grateful for the friendship and guidance of our editors at *Gourmet* magazine, for whom we write our "Roadfood" column. It was they who first sent us to Edisto and who continue to inspire us to discover great places and to write about them. Thanks especially to Ruth Reichl, James Rodewald, and "Doc" Willoughby.

We never hit the road without our virtual companions at Roadfood.com—Steve Rushmore Sr., Stephen Rushmore and Kristin Little, Cindy Keuchle, and Marc Bruno—who constantly fan the flames of appetite and discovery along America's highways and byways.

Thanks also to agent Doe Coover for her tireless work on our behalf and to Jean Wagner, Jackie Willing, Mary Ann Rudolph, and Ned Schankman for making it possible for us to travel in confidence that all's well at home.

Introduction

We don't know of another restaurant where the table setting includes bags of raw grits. The Old Post Office is renowned for grits prepared Lowcountry style, meaning they are long-and-slow-cooked, attaining a pleasant rugged texture but a delicious creamy quality from all the butter and milk they absorb. They come alongside virtually every meal served here, and they are especially wonderful as part of that favorite Lowcountry duet, shrimp and grits.

Grits bags on the table are important not only because the grits at The Old Post Office taste so good but because grits are fundamental to Lowcountry cooking, and here is a restaurant where the food traditions of the region are honored with brio. Ask any food-savvy

person from Edisto, Charleston, or beyond where to eat meals that sing of South Carolina's coastal culture, and chances are good you will be directed to this unlikely place on Edisto Island.

Compared to the rest of Edisto, it is a fairly fancy venue. Its character was established in our minds during our first dinner here by a sound system that was playing chic small-band music, the sort that was on the soundtracks of French new wave movies of the early 1960s. But stylish ambience in no way detracts from the bedrock authenticity of the plates of food that emerge from the kitchen of chef Philip Bardin. Philip rejoices in provender that is as local as can be: oysters straight from oysterman "Mr. Percy," vegetables from the island's fertile soil, and those grits—stone-ground especially for The Old Post Office.

Philip likes nothing more than talking about Edisto's unique personality and relating that personality to the food he cooks. He even credits the especially good flavors of so much of what he serves to the fact that sea breezes waft over the island, infusing groceries with a subtle saline zest. But there is more to The Old Post Office's extraordinary food than excellent ingredients. Chef Bardin is no naïf; a well-trained and sophisticated hand in the kitchen, he applies culinary savvy in a way that puts his Lowcountry fare in a class by itself. Undeniably true to cooking traditions that go back centuries, meals served in this restaurant also offer a modern-day perspective on that kitchen heritage. That unique combination of authenticity and invention makes The Old Post Office a dining experience like none other.

It is an unlikely setting for brilliant meals, an hour's drive from the culinary erudition of Charleston on an island known for its rustic charms. On the way to nowhere (except the beach), it is a true Destination Restaurant, a beacon of good eating in the Lowcountry. Treasured by locals as well as culinary pilgrims, it offers peerless cuisine in a setting that radiates the charm of Edisto's bygone days.

Edisto Island, South Carolina

Edisto has its own time zone, to which residents sometimes knowingly refer as Edislow time. This is not a type-A island, and it is no place for those who charge through life. No one drives too fast and nothing is rushed. As you cruise over the soaring McKinley Washington Jr. Bridge into a landscape of tall grasses and exotic birds, it feels like you have gone a long, long way from the bustling City of Charleston, which is in fact less than an hour's drive away. While Highway 174 that leads into Edisto is a modern, well-paved two-lane road, when you stray from it beyond the bridge, chances are good you will find yourself on a dirt road shaded by live oaks or on a sunlit beach by the sea. While the "business district" of Edisto Beach has a handful of modern stores and amenities, even these operate at a different pace. When we paid a visit to the one public gym on the island, known as the Jungle Gym (because it is on Jungle Road), a brisk workout on the Stairmaster seemed more relaxing than exhausting; and we noted that even the few resident power-lifters hoisted weights with an attitude that could only be called contemplative. Afterwards, at the coffee shop next door, the selection of an espresso drink or a snack became the excuse to stop and chat and discuss coffee and pastries with the forthcoming barrista.

"There are not many places left like Edisto," said Charlie White, proprietor of the Edisto Beach Café, a homespun diner that is nearly as far as you can go on the island before you hit ocean. The café is where a lot of locals come for breakfast and to linger over coffee; and because it is at the corner of the parking lot adjacent to the Piggly Wiggly supermarket, it is a convenient place to stop for lunch before or after grocery shopping. As we stood at Charlie's cash register paying for shrimp burgers (piles of grilled shrimp and caramelized onions piled into a hamburger bun) he explained the pleasure of life on the underdeveloped barrier island: "We're off the beaten path and we like it that way."

Although Edisto (pronounced ED-isto) is not a secret, and a bridge has linked it to the mainland since the thirties, it remains remarkably separate. It hasn't one big-name fast-food franchise; a Burger King opened a while ago but survived barely a year. There are no traffic lights and no motels, and the only theme-park attraction on the seaward side of the intracoastal waterway is a modest serpentarium that provides a place to view many different kinds of reptiles. A few decades ago, Edisto's government restricted the height of all houses to forty feet or less, including the chimney.

Listen to a native Edistonian and you can hear that even the way people speak sets them apart. The language is English, of course— English with a South Carolina accent. But as is true of other Gullah tongues with roots in West Africa, there is a tune to the way people talk that you don't hear inland. Conversations among the locals aren't exactly sung, but they are unmistakably musical.

An eight-by-twelve mile delta that is defined by the Atlantic Ocean and the North and South Edisto Rivers, the island takes its name from the Edistow Indians, for whom it was home when French Huguenots and Spanish explorers began to make their way into the new world in the mid-sixteenth century. The Edistows were weakened by battles with other tribes and by diseases brought by the Europeans, and the tribe is now extinct; but there remains a shell mound on the beach that anthropologists believe was used by them as a ceremonial site. It was the Edistows who "sold" the island to the Earl of Shaftesbury in 1674; after that, English settlers tried to grow rice (with little success because of brackish water).

Only temporarily daunted by Spanish pirates, who burned their homes to the ground in the 1680s, settlers subsequently grew indigo, of which the British Empire needed near-endless supplies for denim work clothes. After the War of Independence turned England into a least-favored trading partner and indigo an unviable crop in the new United

States, local planters turned to Sea Island Cotton. It is said that this long-staple cotton from Edisto was the silkiest in the world; and plantation owners on the island became enormously wealthy growing it and selling it to France.

Profitable cotton growing depended on slavery. Prior to the Civil War, the population of the island was 250 whites and 3,000 African-American slaves; and while cotton returned as a vital crop even after emancipation and the cataclysmic destruction visited by Sherman's troops, it was attacked by an even more deadly enemy, the boll weevil. By the early 1920s, the island's cotton fields had been decimated. It was then resourceful Edistonians began planting their fecund soil with vegetables. And today, the vegetables of Edisto have a reputation for goodness that echoes the glory once brought by cotton and indigo.

While Edisto does have clusters of modern homes and condos, the island never experienced the kind of widespread development that transformed such once-paradisiacal enclaves as Hilton Head. Today, its abundance of wildlife has become a major reason it will likely remain so serene. Because its palmetto-shaded beach is the nesting place for endangered loggerhead turtles from May through autumn, disruptive activities are perforce restrained: no toys or picnic gear may be left on the sand at night, terrapin harassment is punishable by a $20,000 fine, and waterfront residents must keep lights off or drapes drawn after dark so the shoreline remains tranquil enough for the three-hundred pound terrapins to drag themselves onto the sand and lay their eggs in peace. A citizen-volunteer "Turtle Patrol" keeps a lookout for unleashed dogs who might disturb the nests. For visiting human beings, all this vigilance on behalf of the terrapins creates a refuge from stress where basking in peace and quiet is a way of life.

· APPETIZERS ·

Fried Oysters

Firecracker Oysters

Oysters with Caviar

Store Creek Baked Oysters

Oysters with Spinach & Pastry

Fried Shrimp

Stuffed Bacon-Wrapped Shrimp

Shrimp Pâte

Pecan-Coated Shrimp Pâte

Rice Cakes Stuffed with Shrimp Pâte

Fried Ripe Red Tomatoes

Pickled Shrimp

Grits Cakes

"Hominy Cannelloni" on Wilted Greens

Goat Cheese Baguette

Onion Sausage with Black Bean Sauce

Pimiento Cheese

Duck Liver Mousse

Grilled Portobello Pizza

Baked Brie with Grilled Peaches

Oyster & Spinach Dip

Brodie Crab Dip

Watermelon with Country Ham & Blue Cheese

FRIED OYSTERS

South Carolina's Lowcountry boasts some of the finest oysters in the world. They are harvested September through April.

4	*cups peanut oil*
24	*oysters, shucked and in their own liquor*
4	*cups Seafood Breading (page 100)*

In a high-side saucepan on medium-high heat bring the oil up to a temperature of 350°F to 375°F. Check your temperature with a candy thermometer. (Some appliances, such as a Waring Pro Deep Fryer or a Euro-Pro, work well if you do not want to mess with a pan.)

Drain the oysters and dredge them with the breading mix. Carefully add them to the hot oil, cook until crispy and golden—about 1 minute—and retrieve them with a slotted spoon. You can rest them on paper towels. Serve immediately with fresh lemon wedges. Serve six per person.

MAKES 4 SERVINGS

Variation: Here is a recipe Philip developed for late, beloved friend Harold Meggett. It is his simple variation of the Fried Oysters. After dredging, immediately toss the fried oysters in a hot, nonstick pan, and splash and coat with ¼ cup of your favorite hot sauce. At The Old Post Office, we are devoted to Frank's Original Hot Sauce. Serve immediately and watch people sweat.

FIRECRACKER OYSTERS

Firecracker Oysters gets its name because it is a fiercely hot dish, guaranteed to sing reveille on the palates of all who love hot food.

4	cups peanut oil
24	oysters, shucked and in their own liquor
4	cups Seafood Breading (page 100)
1	cup Firecracker Sauce (page 83)

In a high-side saucepan on medium-high heat bring the oil up to a temperature of 350°F to 375°F. Check your temperature with a candy thermometer. (Some appliances, such as a Waring Pro Deep Fryer or a Euro-Pro, work well if you do not want to mess with a pan.)

Drain the oysters and dredge them with the breading mix. Carefully add them to the hot oil, cook until crispy and golden—about 1 minute—and retrieve them with a slotted spoon. While frying the oysters, heat the Firecracker Sauce in a frying pan. Toss in the crispy, fried oysters and coat evenly. Serve hot with crackers or toast.

MAKES 4 SERVINGS

OYSTERS WITH CAVIAR

Looking for an hors d'oeuvre that is simple, elegant, and romantic? Serve oysters with just a dab of sour cream . . . and plenty of good Champagne. This dish must be served icy cold.

24	*oysters, freshly shucked*
6	*teaspoons caviar*
6	*teaspoons sour cream*
	Juice of 1 lemon

Shuck the oysters and leave them in the half shell on a tray of ice. Top each oyster with ½ teaspoon sour cream and ½ teaspoon caviar. Squeeze the lemon entirely over the oysters and serve three per person.

MAKES 8 SERVINGS

STORE CREEK BAKED OYSTERS

I do not care for a lot of fuss when it comes to oysters, especially oysters from Edisto," says Philip Bardin. " But oysters from Edisto aren't available in warm weather months, and so Philip suggests, "This recipe works well for lesser-flavored ones and can be served confidently all year." He describes the dish as "rich and elegant and extremely popular."

12	large oysters, shucked in the half shell
1	cup Old Post Office Crab Cake Mixture (page 133)
½	cup grated Gruyere cheese

Preheat the oven to 500°F. Place the oysters (in their shells) on a baking sheet and top each oyster with a heaping tablespoon of crab mixture. Then top with the cheese in the same manner. Bake for about 15 minutes or until the cheese has melted. Serve three per person.

MAKES 4 SERVINGS

Note: If you are impatient like I am, you can pop the whole thing under a hot broiler and keep watch for the same result.

OYSTERS WITH SPINACH & PASTRY

Philip was always taught that true Oysters Rockefeller do not contain spinach, yet most concoctions do. This is an elegant dish sure to please the Rockefeller fans.

1	tablespoon olive oil
1	tablespoon butter
6	cups washed and trimmed fresh spinach
1	tablespoon Michel Mix (page 96)
	Salt and pepper
12	freshly shucked oysters
½	tablespoon fresh lemon juice
1	tablespoon Pernod
1	tablespoon heavy cream
½	cup grated Parmesan cheese
1	(10-count) can biscuit dough, rolled out to cover an 8-inch-square casserole dish

Preheat the oven to 400°F. Heat the oil in a sauté pan over high heat and add the butter. Sauté the spinach and Michel Mix quickly, adding a little salt and pepper. After just a few minutes on high heat, remove the spinach, and press and strain the liquid, returning it to the sauté pan. Line the spinach in an oval casserole dish, making sure all of the liquid is strained off. Dot the spinach with oysters evenly in the casserole. To the remaining liquid, add the lemon juice, Pernod, and heavy cream, and reduce over high heat until thick, about 3 minutes. Remove from the heat and stir in the grated Parmesan. Pour this liquid over the spinach and oysters slowly and evenly. Top the casserole with rolled-out biscuit dough, overlapping the edges of the dish. Bake until golden, about 12 minutes.

MAKES 4 SERVINGS

FRIED SHRIMP

Shrimp caught near Edisto Island are legendary for their remarkable flavor. Frying them in a light breading mix allows the color (and flavor) of the shrimp to shine through. Philip suggests serving them with nothing more than cocktail and/or tartar sauce.

	Peanut or cottonseed oil for frying
12	*fresh jumbo shrimp, peeled, deveined, and split, with the tail left on*
2	*cups Seafood Breading (page 100)*

Preheat a skillet with the oil until the oil reaches a temperature of 375°F. Simply coat the shrimp evenly with the breading mix to yield a light coating. Fry for exactly 1 minute, remove, and drain.

MAKES 2 SERVINGS

STUFFED BACON-WRAPPED SHRIMP

While bacon-wrapped shrimp is a popular dish in many Charleston restaurants and homes, Philip Bardin is no great fan of it. Still, he says, "Our version is a winner."

12	*fresh shrimp, split, with tails left on*
1	*cup Old Post Office Crab Cake mixture (page 133)*
12	*pieces high quality, thinly sliced bacon, cut in half*

Preheat the oven to 450°F. Fill the shrimp with the crab mixture, and wrap them individually with the half bacon strips. Pierce through the wrapped shrimp with toothpicks. Place the shrimp on a baking sheet, and bake for about 12 minutes, turning once so they will cook evenly.

MAKES 4 SERVINGS

Note: You can also coat these shrimp in breading mixture, and fry just like you would the Fried Shrimp (page 12)—fry for only 3 minutes instead of 1 minute. The fried method is by far the easiest.

SHRIMP PÂTE

Shrimp Pâte stands well on its own or chilled and served with toast points. It can be spread on grilled bread and served warm, or you can shoot the lights out by frying it (see Pecan-Coated Shrimp Pâte, page 15).

1	tablespoon olive oil
1	shallot, minced
1	teaspoon balsamic vinegar
¼	cup dry white wine
12	large shrimp
2	tablespoons Firecracker Sauce (page 83)
1	pound softened cream cheese

In a saucepan heat the olive oil over medium heat and soften the shallot. When translucent and tender (a few minutes), add the balsamic vinegar and white wine. Add the shrimp and Firecracker Sauce, and cook on high heat until the shrimp are cooked thoroughly, about 5 minutes. Strain all the ingredients and let the shrimp stand for about 5 minutes. (It is important to save the liquid to use with the Shrimp Tomato Cream Sauce recipe on page 82.) With the steel blade in your food processor, mix the strained shrimp and blend with the cream cheese. The best way to do this is break off the cream cheese in pieces and add them gradually while the processor is running. When all is blended, the mixture can be placed in a mold for later or scooped out with an ice cream scoop after it is chilled.

MAKES 8 TO 10 SERVINGS

PECAN-COATED SHRIMP PÂTE

It is easier to make Pecan-Coated Shrimp Pâte in a deep-fryer, but it also can be done in a frying pan, like fried oysters or shrimp. It is a little tricky—the oil must be the exactly right temperature. Don't crowd the pan—it is a recipe well worth mastering.

	Peanut oil for deep frying
2	(2-ounce) scoops Shrimp Pâte (page 14), well chilled and very firm
	Egg wash (2 beaten eggs and ½ cup milk blended well)
1½	cups Pecan Flour (page 99)

Fill a heavy saucepan (or a Fry Daddy) with the oil and heat to high. Dip the scoops of Shrimp Pâte in the egg wash, coating them evenly, and then dust them generously in the pecan flour. To be on the safe side, you can repeat this process. Fry the shrimp, watching it constantly. As soon as the scoops are browned on the outside (usually just 1 or 2 minutes), drain and serve immediately. A slotted spoon is ideal for removing the shrimp.

MAKES 4 SERVINGS

Note: If the oil starts making a lot of noise, it may be that the pâte is leaking, and it has been left in the oil too long. This is an "eyes and ears" recipe. We like to serve this with Shrimp Tomato Cream Sauce (page 82) and toasted slices of French bread.

The Old Post Office

The Old Post Office really is Edisto's old post office. Known to long-time islanders as "The Store" because it shared the building with a general store and gas station owned by Willie Bailey (who was also the mail carrier), it is where Edistonians have always come together to say hello and to exchange news. Back in the days when the island was accessible only by ferry, mail delivery was a tremendously crucial connection to the mainland, and islanders knew the exact times during the week when the mail would be put up—these moments being valued occasions for meeting one another at The Store. Edisto had no town square, but it had The Old Post Office, and here gathered citizens of all stripes: fishermen and seashell collectors, farm owners and farm workers.

Chef Philip Bardin recalls that in the early 1980s when he was employed at a local resort, plans were afoot to move The Old Post Office. "At that time, the island was virtually undiscovered," says Philip, recalling just how deeply citizens valued its remoteness. For full-time residents and regular visitors, Edisto was a place to get away from life's stresses, far from most of what constitutes modern life . . . including interesting restaurants. Despite Edisto's relative isolation, Bardin sensed that there was a place and a need for a restaurant that served more sophisticated food than was available in the area.

Encouraged by a friend named Mary Frampton, Philip teamed up with David Gressette, a neighbor on Edisto Beach, and they hatched plans to create a unique eatery on the post office site.

Aside from the dubious commercial viability of running a successful foodservice establishment on a distant piece of real estate, the very creation of the space was a formidable challenge. This was no matter of redecorating and moving in. "The building was a wreck," Philip remembers. "It was eaten by termites. We signed the lease and when I walked in, I literally put my foot through the floor. We had to tear it down to the foundation and start all over."

The restaurant opened in May 1988. A good review by the dining critic at the *Charleston Post & Courier* alerted adventurous eaters from beyond the island, and because Edisto's tranquil air attracted travel writers, articles soon began appearing in the national press singing hosannas to the wonderful food and gracious dining room.

For all its fame, The Old Post Office remains what this particular plot of land always has been: a gathering place for Edistonians. We well remember our first dinner in the comfortable dining room. We relished seats in earshot of a table at which sat twelve stylish women who are all members of a southern social club called the Red Hat Society because they wear bright red hats (and in some cases, bright red dresses to match) whenever they get together. On other occasions, we've seen plenty of table-hopping among those who eat here on a regular basis as well as ebullient camaraderie among the restaurant staff and its regular clientele. Stylish and important as its cuisine may be, The Old Post Office is very much a locals' restaurant.

RICE CAKES STUFFED WITH SHRIMP PÂTE

Requiring no fry-kettle mastery, Shrimp Pâte-Stuffed Rice Cakes are an easy-to-make hors d'oeuvre.

2	*cups leftover cooked rice (overcooked risotto is ideal)*
2	*tablespoons Shrimp Pâte (page 14)*
	Egg wash (2 beaten eggs and 1 cup milk blended well)
2	*cups Pecan Flour (page 99)*
2	*tablespoons butter*

Form eight small, thin cakes with leftover, cold rice. On four of these cakes, place 1 tablespoon of the pâte on the top. Take the remaining cakes and top the pâte until you have four pâte-stuffed cakes. Take the whole cake in your hand and gently, yet firmly, reshape it. Dip each cake in the egg wash and coat liberally with the pecan flour. In a nonstick pan, heat the butter over medium high heat, and sauté the cakes for about 2 minutes on each side until brown and crispy.

MAKES 4 SERVINGS

FRIED RIPE RED TOMATOES

Philip Bardin says, "*Fried Green Tomatoes* is one of my favorite movies of all time. Unfortunately, that is the end of my love affair with the term, and I have never quite understood the recent worship of anything with green tomatoes. To defend my unpopular position, I often send out this wonderful dish, made with *ripe* tomatoes."

4	(1-inch-thick) ripe, fresh tomato slices (use a Better Boy or Good Girl)
	Salt and pepper
	Egg wash (2 beaten eggs and 1 cup milk blended well)
1	cup grated Parmesan cheese
½	cup gluten flour
	Butter or olive oil for sautéing
	Juice of 1 lemon

Sprinkle the tomatoes with salt and pepper. Dip the tomatoes briefly in the egg wash and coat with the Parmesan cheese. Then dust them lightly with the flour. In a nonstick pan heat the butter or olive oil over medium-high heat, and sauté the tomatoes until nice and brown, a few minutes each side. Serve the tomatoes on a plate with a squeeze of fresh lemon juice on top.

MAKES 2 SERVINGS

PICKLED SHRIMP

Pickled shrimp are served throughout the Lowcountry. Serve them The Old Post Office way: Accompany the shrimp with pickled okra or fresh chilled asparagus.

40	fresh large shrimp, boiled and chilled
1	large onion, thinly sliced
1	red pepper, thinly sliced
4	garlic cloves, thinly sliced
8	bay leaves
12	whole allspice
1	teaspoon mustard seeds, cooked in oil, drained, and cooled
2	teaspoons celery seeds
1	cup olive oil
¼	cup red wine vinegar
	Juice of 1 lemon

Peel and devein the shrimp leaving the tails on. Put the shrimp in a container or jar with the onion, pepper, garlic, bay leaves, allspice, mustard seeds, celery seeds, olive oil, vinegar, and lemon juice. Stir gently and refrigerate. Can be served after a minimum 12-hour chill, and they should remain delicious for 10 days.

MAKES 4 SERVINGS

GRITS CAKES

Grits cakes often make an appearance at The Old Post Office in various forms. Philip believes a whole book could be done on the many ways the restaurant has served them over the years. The following is his basic recipe and some alternate suggestions.

2	cups O.P.O. Grits (page 108), cooked and chilled
2	tablespoons butter
	Egg wash (2 beaten eggs and 1 cup milk blended well)
1	cup Pecan Flour (page 99)

Form four cakes with your hands from the chilled grits or use leftover grits. Or pour cooked, hot grits in a small, narrow-side pan, and then chill and cut the mixture with a biscuit cutter. No matter which way you prefer, make sure the cakes are the same size. Melt the butter over medium-high heat in a nonstick sauté pan. Dip the cakes in the egg wash, and dust liberally with plenty of Pecan Flour (you can use regular flour if you like). Sauté the cakes for about 2 minutes on each side or until golden brown. These are excellent with Aunt Min's Gravy (page 97) or our Country Ham Gravy (page 98).

MAKES 4 SERVINGS

Variation: My favorite way to finish Grits Cakes off is to top them with goat cheese while they are still in the pan. Melt the cheese under a hot broiler or in the hot sauté pan with the lid on for about 1 minute. You can also top this with hollandaise sauce for a rich and totally non-spa food experience.

"HOMINY CANNELLONI" ON WILTED GREENS

In the restaurant business you get customers with all kinds of special tastes and diets. Whenever Philip is confronted by a lacto-ovo vegetarian not fond of grits, he says, "Hominy cannelloni wows them every time."

8	tablespoons hot, cooked O.P.O. Grits (page 108)
2	lasagna noodles (sheets), cooked, chilled, and cut in half
½	cup grated mozzarella cheese
	Freshly ground black pepper

Preheat the oven to 450°F. Put 1 tablespoon grits on the lower part of each half lasagna noodle. Spread evenly (and obviously the thicker the grits the better). Top with ⅛ cup grated mozzarella on each half noodle. (You can also use fresh mozzarella pinched and dotted on top, or any other cheese you like.) Roll up the lasagna noodles, keeping as much of the contents in as possible. Place the noodles on an oiled baking sheet. Season with the black pepper to taste, and bake in the oven for about 5 minutes. Since everything is essentially already cooked, the most important thing is not to burn the noodles. Place each "cannelloni" on a bed of wilted greens.

MAKES 4 SERVINGS

Note: This dish commands a glass of light and dry Italian white wine.

GOAT CHEESE BAGUETTE

The Old Post Office kitchen begins with a par-baked baguette, but a fully-baked French bread, sourdough, or Cuban loaf works equally as well. Ashed French Montrachet goat cheese is ideal if you can find it.

2	*(6-inch) baguettes (or 8 thick bread slices)*
1	*(9-ounce) goat cheese log*
2	*tablespoons herbes de Provence*
	Olive oil

Have a hot broiler ready. With the palm of your hand, mash down on the baguette to flatten it evenly. (If you are using thick bread slices, this is not necessary, but lightly toast them first.) Cut the goat cheese log into eight rings (a little over 1 ounce each). Put four rings on top of each baguette. Sprinkle 1 tablespoon of the herbes de Provence on top of each baguette. Top with healthy drizzles of olive oil, and broil until the exposed edges of the bread are well toasted and the cheese is thoroughly softened and almost tanned. Cut each baguette in half. This dish is excellent with pickled shrimp.

MAKES 2 SERVINGS

ONION SAUSAGE WITH BLACK BEAN SAUCE

Philip says, "I would love to give out our onion sausage recipe, but I cannot get it myself, since it is faithfully made for us by Lee's Sausage Company in Orangeburg, South Carolina, and is a family secret." Lee's is typical of the great small processing plants throughout the country.

	Olive oil
2	*pounds rope-style Italian or onion sausage*
1	*medium onion, sliced*
1	*cup Black Bean Soup (page 43)*
1	*tablespoon sour cream*
1	*tablespoon Firecracker Sauce (page 83)*

Preheat the oven to 500°F. In a heavy sauté pan heat the olive oil, and cook the sausage over medium-high heat, turning frequently to brown. When brown on all sides (this takes just a few minutes), bake it on a sheet pan in the oven for 8 to 10 minutes. Remove and let the sausage stand at room temperature. With the hot drippings in the sauté pan, cook the onion until tender. Add the soup and simmer until heated through. Divide this sauce among four plates, and garnish with small dollops of the sour cream and several drops of the Firecracker Sauce. Cut the sausage into quarters and put a piece on each plate.

MAKES 4 SERVINGS

Note: This makes a great appetizer or a main course with fresh steamed rice.

PIMIENTO CHEESE

Philip describes the late Alice Marks as "one of the most storied of the grand dames of Charleston. She made the best pimiento cheese in town, and here is the closest I have figured to her recipe." Pimiento cheese is a staple appetizer in Southern homes.

1	pound sharp cheddar cheese, grated
1	medium onion, grated
¼	pound cream cheese, cut into the smallest cubes possible
1	tablespoon sweet pickle relish
6	cornichons (small tart pickles), minced
6	large stuffed Spanish olives, minced
1	roasted red pepper, cubed (you can use canned, diced pimiento if you must)
1	tablespoon Hellmann's mayonnaise (or very thick homemade)
1	tablespoon Dijon mustard
	Dash of cayenne

In a mixing bowl, fold the cheddar, onion, cream cheese, relish, cornichons, olives, red pepper, mayonnaise, mustard, and cayenne together and refrigerate. A skilled user of the old box cheese grater can actually grate the cream cheese and the onion alternatively for ease.

MAKES 8 TO 10 SERVINGS

Note: We serve this in scoops with crackers and cornichons. It is also great on a summer day with pickled shrimp and boiled peanuts.

DUCK LIVER MOUSSE

If the duck livers are fresh, mousse made from them will be the first to be eaten on any plate of assorted appetizers. In fact, Philip warns, "If this dish is delivered as a gift to a friend's party, be sure the person carrying it is trustworthy. Otherwise, have it sent by armored car."

6	duck livers
4	tablespoons Courvoisier (cognac)
½	stick butter
1	tablespoon Michel Mix (page 96)
5	ounces goat cheese, softened
5	ounces cream cheese, softened
1	teaspoon kosher salt
1	teaspoon freshly grated black pepper

Marinate the livers in Courvoisier overnight. In a sauté pan, melt the butter. Drain the livers, saving the liquid. Sauté the livers and Michel Mix over low heat for 5 to 7 minutes. At the finish, turn the heat to high, and pour in the reserved liquid, which should flame up. Remove from heat and let stand for 10 minutes. In a food processor with the steel knife, blend the livers and juices with the cheeses, salt, and pepper. You can serve warm, spread on baguettes, or chill for later.

MAKES 6 TO 8 SERVINGS

Note: If you do not like Courvoisier, I have used Madeira, Drambuie, and my personal favorite, pumpkin liqueur (good luck finding that).

GRILLED PORTOBELLO PIZZA

The Old Post Office is set in her ways," Philip says. "I confess to being annoyed at times by vegetarians. However, a call placed one day ahead to warn me often yields the best food served that evening. This is one of the many things I make for my favorite and beloved veggie, Parker Kaufman."

1	cup olive oil
½	cup dry vermouth
4	tablespoons balsamic vinegar
2	large portobello mushrooms
1	tablespoon Firecracker Sauce (page 83) or a tomato sauce
2	teaspoons goat cheese or fresh mozzarella

Mix the oil, vermouth, and vinegar in a large bowl. Add the mushrooms and cover. Marinate for at least 1 hour. Prepare a grill to hot, and grill the mushrooms until tender, turning often, about 5 minutes. Top each mushroom with ½ tablespoon Firecracker Sauce and 1 teaspoon goat cheese. Melt the cheese and cut the mushrooms into quarters, giving the appearance of a small pizza. This is great served with braised greens.

MAKES 4 SERVINGS

BAKED BRIE WITH GRILLED PEACHES

Nothing is more passé than baked Brie accompanied with apples or almonds," Philip declares. "This is a little different. Chef Phil Corr of Atlanticville, who once served me foie gras in pastry with a peach slice, was its inspiration."

2	firm peaches, pitted and cut into eighths
2	(4-inch) puff pastry squares, rolled out
2	small (4-ounce) wheels of Brie
1	egg, beaten

Preheat the oven to 400°F. On a hot grill (or you can broil or sauté) that has been lightly oiled to prevent sticking, grill the peach slices, turning once until just tender, 3 to 4 minutes. Grill marks are a bonus. Place 2 peach slices in the center of each pastry square, and then gently place a Brie round on top of that. Wrap and cover each entire wheel, and turn over onto on a sheet pan. Brush the top of the pastries with the beaten egg for a shiny color, and bake until golden brown, 5 to 7 minutes. Garnish with the remaining grilled peaches.

MAKES 4 SERVINGS

OYSTER & SPINACH DIP

Philip says this intoxicating dip can be served hot or cold. We like it warm, with the freshest possible oysters.

1	tablespoon olive oil
1	tablespoon butter
6	cups washed and trimmed fresh spinach
1	tablespoon Michel Mix (page 96)
	Salt and pepper
12	freshly shucked oysters
½	tablespoon fresh lemon juice
1	tablespoon Pernod
1	tablespoon heavy cream
½	cup grated Parmesan cheese

Preheat the oven to 400°F. Heat the oil in a sauté pan over high heat and add the butter. Sauté the spinach and Michel Mix quickly, adding a little salt and pepper. After just a few minutes on high heat, remove the spinach, and press and strain the liquid. Return the spinach to the sauté pan. Add the oysters, lemon juice, Pernod, and heavy cream, and reduce over high heat until thick, about 3 minutes. Remove from the heat and stir in the grated Parmesan. This can be served hot or chilled.

MAKES 4 SERVINGS

BRODIE CRAB DIP

Down Store Creek from The Old Post Office is a hideaway known as Brodie," Philip says. "It is the headquarters of the Scottish half of my family. My cousin Brenda makes the perfect dip in the kitchen while the Brodie men clean the fresh blue crabs right on the dock."

2	*pounds freshly picked crabmeat with no shells at all*
1	*teaspoon Old Bay Seasoning*
1	*teaspoon lemon juice*
2	*teaspoons prepared horseradish*
1	*tablespoon Hellmann's mayonnaise to bind*

Place in a large mixing bowl the crabmeat, seasoning, lemon juice, horseradish, and mayonnaise. Lightly fold all the ingredients together and chill. Serve with assorted crackers.

MAKES 8 SERVINGS

WATERMELON WITH COUNTRY HAM & BLUE CHEESE

I have been unable to locate the fabulous 'Honey Heart' melons that used to come from Cameron, South Carolina. But sweet watermelon is fine in this 'redneck' version of melon and proscuitto. It is a weird dish," Philip admits, "but it works."

12	*ripe watermelon pieces, seeded, cut in squares, and chilled*
2	*thin country ham slices, grilled or pan fried*
½	*cup crumbled Clemson or buttermilk blue cheese*
¼	*cup fresh cut mint, medium to fine cut*

Arrange the melon on a large plate, making sure that each piece is at least somewhat exposed. Cut the ham slices into narrow strips (try to get about two dozen) and layer over the melon. Sprinkle the blue cheese over this and finish with a sprinkling of the mint.

MAKES 4 SERVINGS

Note: Country ham is available in almost all stores. I like Goodnight Brothers.

Sweetgrass Baskets

Annette King now lives on Edisto, where her husband was born, but she comes from Mt. Pleasant, just north of Charleston; it was there at the age of five that she started to weave the sweetgrass baskets that she now sells outside her home along Highway 174 on the island. Basket stands have been part of the roadside scene in Mt. Pleasant since Highway 174 was paved in the 1930s. And the craft goes far back to the days of the slaves, who brought it with them from West Africa. It has been passed down through the generations from mother to daughter.

Traditionally made from long-bladed sweetgrass, bulrush, long-leaf pine needles, and palmetto leaves, the baskets are beautiful objets d'art

. . . as well as being strong and practical. In the old days, big sturdy ones were used to collect vegetables and grains in the field; some were made to winnow rice; smaller ones, made from the softer grasses, became serving trays and sewing boxes.

Mrs. King told us that sometimes the mood strikes her to make a huge basket, but generally she makes the smaller, more decorative ones. The sweetgrass she uses (formally named *Muhlenbergia filipes*) is soft shades of green, tan, and yellow, and is pliable enough to create sensuously curving handles and rims for the baskets she sells from her stand by the side of the road that leads to Edisto Beach.

· BREADS ·

Old Post Office (O.P.O.) Bread
Bacon & Cheddar Bread
Ginger Croutons
Biscuits
Sweet Potato Biscuits
Skillet Cornbread

OLD POST OFFICE (O.P.O.) BREAD

Before there was a bakery on Edisto Island, Edistonians used to come to the back door of the restaurant to buy loaves of Old Post Office Bread.

1	tablespoon sugar
1	tablespoon salt
3	cups lukewarm water (110°F to 115°F)
2	(¼-ounce) packages active dry yeast
7	to 8 cups hi-gluten bread flour
1	tablespoon olive oil
1	cup fine cracker meal

In a container, mix the sugar and salt in the water, making sure they are completely dissolved. Stir in the yeast, and let stand for a few minutes to be certain the yeast bubbles. Pour the liquid into a mixer with a dough hook attachment, and turn on slow to medium speed. Slowly add 1 cup flour at a time until all the flour forms a ball. Turn off the mixer. With the olive oil, coat the dough ball either with your hands or by just flipping on the mixer a few seconds. Remove the dough hook. Allow the dough ball to rise to nearly double in bulk, 10 to 20 minutes. Push down.

On a table or board, spread out the cup of cracker meal. Place the dough on the meal-covered table or board. Separate it into three parts, and coat the outsides by rolling them in the cracker meal. Preheat the oven to 375°F.

On a baking sheet that is either sprayed with Pam or covered in parchment paper, take each dough section, and hand-stretch it into a loaf about 16 inches long. Keep the loaves several inches apart. Bake for 40 to 45 minutes until golden brown and a hollow sound is made when given a "thump." If your oven has not been calibrated recently, start checking for doneness after 30 minutes. When done, take out the loaves and brush them with butter or olive oil.

MAKES 3 LOAVES, 16 SERVINGS

Note: The dough-making part can be done without a mixer in a mixing bowl with a wooden spoon. Another great tip is to reserve some of the dough, coat it in olive oil, and refrigerate. Use for a future pizza.

BACON & CHEDDAR BREAD

Philip recalls, "When my daughter Rachel was very young, she adored an older, downtown Charleston French chef who did not speak English. He would bring her out 'Bacon Bread.' It is a good way to add oomph to the preceding recipe."

1	recipe O.P.O. Bread (page 35), unbaked and shaped in three sections
36	strips cooked bacon (apple-smoked bacon is ideal), crumbled
2	cups grated sharp Cheddar cheese

Preheat the oven to 375°F. Stretch each loaf out about 16 inches, and roll flat to about a 1-inch height. Sprinkle the crumbled bacon and Cheddar evenly on the flat dough. Tightly roll each piece of dough lengthwise, encasing the bacon and Cheddar. Bake for 40 to 45 minutes, checking for doneness after 30 minutes. Let cool and slice.

MAKES 3 LOAVES, 16 SERVINGS

GINGER CROUTONS

Folks love garlic croutons in salads or garlic toast with dips," Philip says. "For a refreshing change, I like to make croutons with fresh ginger."

1	cup finely chopped fresh ginger
1	teaspoon lemon juice
6	thin slices O.P.O. or French bread
	Olive oil

When chopping the ginger, cut it as small as possible and remove any large, tough fibers. Place the ginger in a mixing bowl and stir in the lemon juice to keep the ginger from discoloring. Preheat the oven to 350°F.

Cut the bread slices in half lengthwise to yield 12 pieces. Rub with the ginger and place the bread on a baking sheet. Drizzle olive oil over the top of each bread piece, and bake until brown around the edges, 7 to 10 minutes. Let stand at room temperature for 10 minutes before serving.

MAKES 2 SERVINGS

BISCUITS

Old Post Office former sous chef Robert Mellette insisted on including biscuits in the bread repertoire, and according to Philip, he made some fine ones. "An unair-conditioned kitchen made them a morning labor of love."

2	cups White Lily self-rising flour
1	teaspoon baking powder (use a non-aluminum brand like Rumford's)
1	teaspoon salt
1	tablespoon sugar
¼	teaspoon baking soda
½	cup butter-flavored shortening
¾	cup buttermilk

Preheat the oven to 375°F. Combine the flour, baking powder, salt, sugar, and baking soda in a bowl and mix well. Tear the shortening into bits and add to the bowl. Roll the dry ingredients and shortening bits in the palms of your hands by rubbing them together, making "beads" throughout the mixture. When all is well mixed, slowly stir in the buttermilk until just blended. Allow the dough to rise, about 10 minutes, and turn out on a floured table or board. Spread the dough into a 1-inch-thick rectangle and carefully fold over in half. Do not knead or fuss over the dough. Cut dough with a 3- or 4-inch biscuit cutter and put biscuits on a baking sheet lined with parchment paper. Bake for 10 to 12 minutes until golden, and then brush with melted butter.

MAKES 4 SERVINGS, ABOUT 2 BISCUITS PER SERVING

SWEET POTATO BISCUITS

The late Bill Neal was instrumental in bringing Southern food to national prominence," Philip recalls. "He had a profound influence on our restaurant. Sweet potato biscuits were one of my favorites of his creations."

1	medium sweet potato, peeled and cut in thick pieces
2	cups water
2	tablespoons brown sugar
2	tablespoons honey
1	teaspoon salt
1	teaspoon white pepper
1	recipe biscuit dough (page 38)

Boil the sweet potato in the water with the sugar, honey, salt, and pepper until very tender, about 15 minutes. Strain and purée. This should yield about 1½ cups. Allow to cool. Add the sweet potato mix to the biscuit dough, stirring very gently before turning the dough out onto a board. Spread the dough into a 1-inch-thick rectangle and carefully fold over in half. Do not knead or fuss over the dough. Cut dough with a 3- or 4-inch biscuit cutter and put biscuits on a baking sheet lined with parchment paper. Bake for 10 to 12 minutes until golden, and then brush with melted butter.

MAKES 6 SERVINGS, ABOUT 2 BISCUITS PER SERVING

SKILLET CORNBREAD

The With These Hands craft gallery has been a next-door neighbor of The Old Post Office since it opened. Philip sends Skillet Cornbread to the ladies there, especially when they complain of being driven crazy by the aroma of the restaurant's morning baking. His own favorite way to eat the cornbread is drizzled with sorghum.

1	large egg
2	cups buttermilk
1	tablespoon melted duck fat or butter
1¾	cups cornmeal
1	teaspoon salt
1	teaspoon baking powder
1	teaspoon baking soda
1	teaspoon sugar

Preheat the oven to 450°F. In a mixing bowl combine the egg and buttermilk well. Stir in the melted fat. In a separate bowl mix together the cornmeal, salt, baking powder, baking soda, and sugar. Add the dry ingredients to the liquid mixture. Spray an 8-inch, cast-iron skillet with nonstick cooking spray and pour in the batter. Bake for about 15 minutes and turn the cornbread out onto a plate. It can be lathered in butter or topped with drizzled honey. Serve with chili, soups, or stews.

MAKES 4 SERVINGS

· SOUPS & SALADS ·

FRAGILE

Black Bean Soup

Oyster Soup

Tourist's Cold Soup

Emerald Potato Soup

Blue Crab Soup

Cure-All Soup

Okra Stew

Clam, Jalapeño & Cheddar Bisque

Shrimp, Spinach & Blue Cheese Bisque

Shrimp & Sweet Corn Chowder

Cherry's Clam & Sausage Chowder

David's O.P.O. House Salad

Fried Oyster Salad

Shrimp Salad

Sea Scallop & Wilted Greens Salad

Boston Lettuce Salad with Toasted Almonds

Racky's Halibut Salad

Duck & Wonton Salad

Elloree Chicken Salad

Tomato & Goat Cheese Stack

Peanut, Honey & Blue Cheese Salad

Buttermilk Blue Cheese & Cider Slaw

BLACK BEAN SOUP

This soup was inspired by a Cuban chef Philip knew as a child.

7	cups chicken or vegetable stock
2	cups dried black beans free of stones, soaked in water overnight
1	cup medium hot salsa (or Firecracker Sauce, page 83)
1	medium onion, minced
1	garlic clove, minced
1	teaspoon cumin
1	teaspoon black pepper
	Sour cream

Bring the stock to a boil. Add the beans, salsa, onion, garlic, cumin, and pepper, and simmer until the beans are tender, about 1½ hours. Stir often. Let stand for 1 hour off the heat, covered, or best of all, place in a slow cooker on low. Taste before serving and add salt if necessary. To serve, put a dollop of sour cream on top.

MAKES 6 SERVINGS

"Mr. Percy" Berry, the Oyster Man

Oysters are a pillar of Lowcountry cooking. They are roasted, eaten raw, and fried; they are combined with pork and made into sausages; they are made into stews and soups. And while oysters are found on local menus year-round, they are at their best between September and April, when oyster men harvest them from creeks and ocean beds. The single dish in The Old Post Office repertoire that we love most is the Oyster Skillet (page 127), the glory of which Philip Bardin attributes to his esteemed oyster man, "Mr. Percy" Berry.

Philip wrote, "If the month has an 'R' in it and it happens to be Thursday, Mr. T. P. ("Mr. Percy") Berry is the most important person on Edisto Island. Local oysters from the surrounding waters are often said to be the best in the world and are worshipped throughout the Lowcountry. The familiar rattle of an old truck is a welcome noise and has been for generations of Edistonians. It is the signal of the arrival of the beloved oysterman, who says, 'I've been messin' with oysters all my life.'

"Born outside the small Lowcountry town of Bowman, Mr. Percy has made the trek to Edisto for decades. Many locals recall his old wooded sideboard truck packed down with vegetables and sometimes seafood. His arrival in the yards of the old clapboard beach houses—

signaled by a hoarse honk—triggered a rush to greet him as he delivered his goods.

"In the fall and spring, Mr. Percy is a lifeline for The Old Post Office, having favored the restaurant with his oysters from its earliest days. The once-a-week ritual begins with a growling, 'How many you want?'"

After Mr. Percy's superior oysters are iced away, Chef Bardin always favors his oysterman with hunks of freshly-baked bread slathered with butter. As Mr. Percy devours his favorite midday snack, he and Bardin kick back and enjoy each other's company, exchanging stories of life on Edisto, yesterday and today.

OYSTER SOUP

Here is the dish to make when you have freshly shucked oysters of outstanding quality, because the integrity of the oysters makes or breaks it. "We are lucky most of the year with our Percy Berry oysters," Philip says. "A quick recipe, this is one of the few soups that is actually better done as close to serving as possible."

1	tablespoon butter
1	small onion or 3 shallots, minced
1	stalk celery, minced
2	tablespoons finely diced carrots
1	garlic clove, minced
1	bay leaf
1	pint fresh oysters in their liquor
2	tablespoons heavy cream

Melt the butter in a medium sauté pan over medium-high heat, and sauté the onion, celery, carrots, garlic, and bay leaf until tender, about 5 minutes. Remove the bay leaf, add the oysters with juice, and stir quickly. When the oysters are just heated through and starting to curl, add the cream. Stir and reduce over high heat for 1 to 2 minutes. Serve immediately.

MAKES 2 TO 4 SERVINGS

TOURIST'S COLD SOUP

Philip Bardin has mixed feelings about tourists to Edisto; while he has been known to make sport of their high black socks with sandals and new mountain bikes strapped to their vehicles, he also credits one with a recipe for cold soup that "blew me away." The tourist was a chef from New York, who concocted this soup after a visit to Miss Pink's vegetable stand down the road. This recipe sounds weird—probably is—but it's wonderful.

1	*large, perfectly ripe cantaloupe*
2	*large, perfectly ripe tomatoes.*

Clean the cantaloupe and cut it into chunks. Skin and seed the tomatoes. Simply purée these two ingredients in the blender. Chill and serve.

MAKES 4 SERVINGS

Note: This is great with freshly ground black pepper and a little mint added.

EMERALD POTATO SOUP

This is similar to a vichyssoise, a rich, creamy potato-and-leek soup that's served cold and garnished with chives.

4	cups chicken stock
3	cups diced potatoes
1	Vidalia onion, chopped
3	cups fresh spinach, cleaned and trimmed
2	teaspoons salt
1	cup heavy cream, optional

Bring the chicken stock to a boil, and simmer the potatoes and onion until the potatoes are tender, about 15 minutes. Add the spinach and salt, and turn off the heat. Chill and then purée the mixture in a blender, adding the cream, if using. This soup is supposed to be served cold.

MAKES 4 SERVINGS

BLUE CRAB SOUP

She-crab soup is one of Charleston's signature dishes, although Philip points out that the original version isn't really all that old. Besides, he much prefers his own Blue Crab Soup.

4	cups water
1	cup white wine
1	lemon, quartered
1	tablespoon seafood seasoning (Old Bay)
4	large, live crabs (2 pounds worth of crabmeat)
½	pound crab roe
3	cups cooked rice
½	cup heavy cream
4	tablespoons good sherry

For the stock bring the water, wine, lemon, and seasoning to a boil in a large pot. You must then cruelly sacrifice the live crabs, put the pot on a low simmer, and cover for about 20 to 30 minutes. With a large mallet, or preferably a large wooden pestle, crush the crabs as finely as you can, and drain the contents, reserving the liquid. This is your soup stock. Put half the crabmeat, half the roe, and the rice in the stock base and heat over medium heat for a few minutes. Purée the mixture in a blender and add the heavy cream. Pour the hot soup in a tureen and add the remaining crab and roe. Salt to taste and add the sherry.

MAKES 4 TO 6 SERVINGS

CURE-ALL SOUP

Any time a member of the staff or a good friend is ailing, Cure-All Soup is what goes out of the back door. Philip declares it is "proven to be effective against colds . . . and is also delicious." If you make a large quantity and have three servings of this per day along with two apples and a salad for a week, you will feel great . . . if only from the weight lost.

4	cups duck or chicken stock
	Juice of 1 lemon
½	cup finely minced fresh ginger
2	garlic cloves (at room temperature), thinly sliced
1	cup diced, cooked chicken, turkey, or duck
1	cup Arborio rice
1	teaspoon kosher salt
1	teaspoon freshly ground black pepper

Bring the stock to a boil, and add the lemon juice, ginger, garlic, chicken, rice, salt, and pepper. Simmer over low heat, stirring from time to time. The soup can be served after about 30 minutes of cooking time, but the longer it simmers, the better. I like to thicken it with 1 to 2 tablespoons cornstarch mixed with a little water to make a slurry.

MAKES 4 SERVINGS

Note: Peel the ginger with a spoon and do not use a food processor to mince it.

OKRA STEW

Like barbecue and politics, okra inspires great passion. You either love it or you hate it. Philip reports that "the *Charleston Post & Courier's* legendary columnist, the late Ashley Cooper (Frank Gilbreth Jr.), once formed an okra haters' society." The okra-hater may or may not be swayed by this recipe, but the okra-lover most certainly will be soothed.

1	large ham bone with a lot of meat still intact
2½	quarts (10 cups) chicken or duck stock
2	pounds okra, cleaned and cut into 1-inch rings
6	ripe tomatoes, seeded and skinned or 2 (14-ounce) cans whole peeled tomatoes
1	onion, chopped coarsely
1	teaspoon dried oregano
1	teaspoon dried thyme
1	tablespoon chopped fresh parsley
	Salt
2	cups shelled boiled peanuts, optional

Bring the ham bone, stock, okra, tomatoes, onion, oregano, thyme, parsley, and salt to a slow simmer for several hours. Remove the ham bone. If any good pieces of ham remain, remove from the bone and toss back in the stew. Simmer for another 30 minutes. If you use the shelled boiled peanuts, add them, and let the stew stand for 20 minutes, covered, off of the heat.

MAKES 6 SERVINGS

Note: The peanuts add the illusion of okra seeds gone mad, taste wonderful, and will possibly convert the okra hater.

CLAM, JALAPEÑO & CHEDDAR BISQUE

You will not find this dish on the menu of The Old Post Office. They quit making it because too many people wanted large quantities to-go for family gatherings. Because the dominant flavors are jalapeño peppers and sharp Cheddar, canned clams are perfectly fine to use . . . especially if you do not tell anyone.

36	*clams, shucked, and with their liquor (or substitute canned)*
4	*cups chicken stock*
3	*medium jalapeño peppers, seeded and diced*
1	*large Vidalia onion, chopped*
¼	*pound butter*
1	*cup flour*
2	*cups grated sharp Cheddar cheese*
1	*cup heavy cream*

Bring the clams, stock, jalapeños, and onion to a boil, and simmer for about 5 minutes in a saucepot. In a separate pot (make sure it is a bit larger than the one in use) prepare a blonde roux by melting the butter and stirring in the flour. (Here is where I break with tradition. I use hi-gluten flour and cook the roux on high heat for just a few minutes.) Add the clam and liquid ingredients to the roux 1 cup at a time. This will be very hot. Stir carefully and rapidly, and add the cheese while stirring. It should melt evenly and perfectly. Turn the heat off and finish with the heavy cream.

MAKES 4 SERVINGS

SHRIMP, SPINACH & BLUE CHEESE BISQUE

Full-flavored chicken stock or good seafood stock is essential to making a very rich bisque, which is so good with toasted French bread.

4	*cups seafood, fish, or chicken stock*
2	*pounds shrimp, cooked and chopped*
4	*cups spinach, cleaned and trimmed*
¼	*pound butter*
1	*cup all-purpose flour*
1	*cup Clemson or buttermilk blue cheese, crumbled*
1	*cup heavy cream*
	Bacon, crisply cooked and crumbled

Bring the stock to a boil and add the shrimp and spinach. Turn off the heat, and let stand while you make the roux. In a separate pot (make sure it is a bit larger than the one in use) prepare a roux by melting the butter and stirring in the flour. Cook the roux on high heat for just a few minutes. This will be very hot. Stir carefully and rapidly. Add the shrimp and spinach mixture to the roux in batches, and add the cheese in batches as well. Turn off and stir in the cream. Top with crumbled bacon.

MAKES 4 SERVINGS

SHRIMP & SWEET CORN CHOWDER

Nothing is better than Edisto sweet corn. It is almost a sin even to cook it. It grows abundantly on the island and is at its best the day it is picked. Philip's grand soup takes full advantage of the nectar of the corn by matching it with local shrimp.

¼	*pound butter*
1	*cup flour*
4	*cups chicken stock*
2	*cups freshly peeled, small creek shrimp or chopped larger shrimp (raw)*
2	*cups Silver Queen corn kernels just off the cob, saving as much juice as possible*
½	*cup diced and cooked country ham*
1	*cup heavy cream*

In a large pot prepare a roux by melting the butter and stirring in the flour. Cook the roux on high heat for just a few minutes. This will be very hot. Stir carefully and rapidly. Set aside. In a separate pot bring the stock to a boil, and add the shrimp, corn, and ham. Return the roux to medium heat. When the shrimp are just turning pink (less than 1 minute), add the mixture to the roux in small batches, stirring constantly. Stir in the cream, and take the stew off the heat when the desired thickness is achieved. The trick is not to overcook the shrimp and, more importantly in this case, the corn.

MAKES 4 SERVINGS

CHERRY'S CLAM & SAUSAGE CHOWDER

If you took a survey of Edistonians and asked them who is the best cook on the island, Cherry Smalls's name would surface immediately," Philip says. "If you threw in a qualifier of who is also the sweetest and sincerest person on this island, you would get the same name. For me, every day is like my birthday because Cherry Smalls is the sous chef at The Old Post Office, and we have known each other for more than twenty years. The Clam Chowder at the restaurant has been passed on to various members of the kitchen clan. When it was Cherry's turn—it became fantastic."

1	quart (4 cups) shucked surf clams with liquor (canned can work)
3	cups chicken stock
3	cups tomato purée
1	pound onion sausage or any rope Italian sausage, cut into medium pieces
1	large onion, minced
1	large carrot, cut in 1-inch cubes
3	Yukon Gold potatoes, scrubbed and cut into 1-inch cubes
1	stalk celery, thinly sliced
1	yellow bell pepper, coarsely chopped
1	red pepper, coarsely chopped
3	tablespoons hot sauce (Frank's Original)
1	tablespoon kosher salt
1	tablespoon dried thyme
2	teaspoons dried oregano

In a large pot over medium-high heat, bring the clams and their liquid, the stock, and the purée to a boil. Add the sausage, onion, carrot, potatoes, celery, bell pepper, red pepper, hot sauce, salt, thyme, and oregano. Simmer for at least 1 hour before serving.

MAKES 8 TO 10 SERVINGS

DAVID'S O.P.O. HOUSE SALAD

The pride of Clemson University in South Carolina, blue cheese is fundamental in the salad that return customers have come to expect at the start of an Old Post Office meal. Philip recalls, "In the early days of the restaurant, we did a different house salad every night. My partner, David Gressette, worked out front and surveyed the comments. As the restaurant grew busier, the salad issue became a problem, and David finally came up with the salad that customers like best. Getting sufficient Clemson blue cheese to make it was a great O.P.O. victory in the early days."

1	head romaine lettuce
2	cups mesclun or spring mix
½	cup freshly grated Parmesan cheese
1	cucumber, thinly sliced
1	bunch red seedless grapes
1	cup fresh pecan pieces
2	Roma tomatoes, thinly sliced
1	small red onion, sliced in thin circles
	O.P.O. House Dressing (page 92)
	Clemson Blue Cheese crumbles

Wash the romaine leaves and pull into pieces without the center rib. Wash and add the mesclun or spring mix to the romaine in a large bowl. This salad is interesting in that the grated Parmesan is used as a seasoning. They are sprinkled over to coat all the leaves first. Then add and arrange the cucumber, grapes, pecans, tomatoes, and onion to suit your fancy. Either top or toss with the O.P.O. House Dressing and sprinkle blue cheese on last.

MAKES 4 SERVINGS

FRIED OYSTER SALAD

We once had a main course salad called a 'Sharpe Salad,' after Bill Sharpe, a great customer and popular Charleston news anchor," Philip recalls. "The salad was loaded with fried seafood and four types of cheeses and became impossible to put together on busy nights. Our Fried Oyster Salad is a descendant of the Sharpe Salad and a must-make once you have mastered the frying pan."

---

24 *Fried Oysters (page 7)*
   Juice of ½ lemon
   Dash of hot sauce (Frank's Original)
   David's O.P.O. House Salad (page 56) without the dressing
   Wasabi Vinaigrette (page 94)

When you fry your oysters this time, do not drain them too thoroughly. After you retrieve them, put them in a pan and toss them in the lemon juice and hot sauce. While they are hot, pour them over the salad, and top with an ample drizzle of the Wasabi Vinaigrette. Serve with grilled garlic bread or even hot hushpuppies.

MAKES 4 SERVINGS

Frying

If the notion of fried shrimp puts you in mind of some tasteless crescent of stringy white meat smothered by a sarcophagus of doughy bread with a greasy crust, eating a shrimp platter in or around Charleston will change your attitude 180 degrees. With the possible exception of Essex River clams on Cape Ann, Massachusetts, there's nothing better fried than South Carolina seafood.

The first reason for this fact is that local shrimp, oysters, and flounder are themselves the best. Shrimp are a fundamental part of local culture, historically sold spiced and ready to eat by vendors at

streetcorner carts. Whether little sweeties caught in local creeks or pink plumpies hauled in with capacious cast nets, shrimp are available in myriad preparations, but the fried shrimp served in local restaurants are unsurpassed. Oysters, too, are a passion, harvested from beds in the Lowcountry's creeks and marshes—delicious raw or roasted, but especially succulent when encased in a fine brittle-fried red-gold crust. And flounder, caught year-round in the waters off the barrier islands, are meaty and substantial enough that frying only accentuates their character.

The other reason fried seafood is so good here is that South Carolina's coastal cooks are masters of the fry kettle. This is a fact we learned one delicious night many years ago when John Martin Taylor, author of *Hoppin' John's Lowcountry Cooking*, took us for fried seafood at the old Edisto Motel dining room. Taylor is a sophisticated gastronome, so we were a little bit surprised when he insisted we get all our seafood fried. But he was right; and the meals we ate that night were a revelation, proof of Taylor's proposition that "Deep frying is an art in the Lowcountry." He writes, "Foods that are deep-fried in clean hot oil or lard are crisper and less greasy than those that are sautéed or pan-fried."

It is fair to say that in this appetizing part of the world, fried food is positively refreshing. Lynne Rossetto Kasper, host of Public Radio's *The Splendid Table*, once declared coastal South Carolina was the only place she's spent a week eating fried things once or even twice a day and wound up actually losing a few pounds!

What we love about the fried shrimp, oysters, and flounder at The Old Post Office is that the crust has real oomph and flavor. This is no featherweight tempura that is all about texture with little taste. The savor and crunch of the fried envelope that surrounds the meat are substantial; and what's inside that red-gold veil are shrimp that are snapping-fresh, Folly Creek oysters with unspeakably luscious marine savor, or big slabs of flounder that flake into steaming white hunks once you crack through the brittle crust with a fork.

SHRIMP SALAD

I have carried this recipe with me every place I have ever worked," Philip says. "It was based on a Windrose Salad that was taught to me by Chef Max Von Salis of Switzerland."

24	*boiled shrimp, peeled, deveined, and cut into bite-size pieces*
	Dash of lemon juice
	Dash of tarragon vinegar
1	*teaspoon salt*
1	*teaspoon white pepper*
1	*teaspoon curry*
1	*teaspoon fresh mint*
1	*teaspoon fresh dill*
1	*teaspoon sweet pickle relish*
1	*teaspoon dill pickle relish*
1	*teaspoon high quality or homemade mayonnaise, to bind.*

Put the shrimp in a salad bowl, and add the lemon juice and tarragon vinegar. Then add the salt, white pepper, curry, mint, dill, sweet relish, and dill relish in the exact order listed. The list of ingredients seems suspect, but the result is outstanding. Bind lightly with the mayonnaise, just enough to bind the ingredients together. Serve in an avocado or melon half or ripe tomato star.

MAKES 2 TO 4 SERVINGS

SEA SCALLOP & WILTED GREENS SALAD

One supermarket bag of spring mix or mesclun is what you need here. Philip says, "I make this salad exclusively for Casey Gressette, my partner's wife and one of my dearest friends. The greens reduce to where there is a lot of nutrition per serving. The recipe is for one salad."

4	large sea scallops
2	tablespoons O.P.O. House Dressing (page 92)
1	(4-ounce) bag spring or mesclun mix
	Lemon
	Sprinkle of kosher salt
	Freshly ground black pepper
	Wasabi Vinaigrette (page 94)

Heat a large saucepan over medium-high heat and sear the scallops for 2 to 3 minutes. Remove them from the pan and add the dressing. Heat the dressing on high. Throw in the greens, adding a squeeze of the lemon, the salt, and pepper, and allow the various leaves to reduce. After a quick flash-fry for about 30 to 45 seconds, put the greens on a warm plate, and arrange the scallops on the greens. A drizzle of Wasabi Vinaigrette to finish is a nice touch. Serve with olives and Ginger Croutons (page 37).

MAKES 2 SERVINGS

BOSTON LETTUCE SALAD WITH TOASTED ALMONDS

When he was a chef at the Loft Oyster Bar in Columbia, South Carolina, Philip made a Boston lettuce salad with toasted almonds. It has remained his favorite salad ever since. He notes, " The idea is to make a flower-like effect with perfect and large Boston lettuce arranged on each plate. The leaves act like smaller plates and the other ingredients can rest in them."

2	heads Boston lettuce
½	cup slivered almonds, freshly toasted in the oven and still warm
	Juice of 1 lemon
	Walnut oil
	Raspberry vinegar
	Black pepper

Wash the whole lettuce leaves in a clean sink or large bowl with ice water. This will make any sand sink to the bottom. Be careful not to tear the leaves. Remove and dry them thoroughly. Arrange the leaves on large plates for service, and put a pinch of toasted almonds in each leaf "pocket". Give a splash of lemon juice over each salad, and finish all off with very light drizzles of walnut oil and light colorful dashes of raspberry vinegar and black pepper to taste. This simple but elegant salad is wonderful with Ginger Croutons (page 37) and/or garlic bread and fresh fruit.

MAKES 4 SERVINGS

RACKY'S HALIBUT SALAD

Philip says, "Luckily for me, one of my main fishmongers, Racky Hays of Crosby's Seafood, happens to be a degenerate horseplayer like me and one of my best friends. We like to take chances. Occasionally when the weather is bad, I'll have him bring fish not native to these waters as long as the quality is outstanding. This one is a winner."

	David's O.P.O. House Salad (page 56)
4	very fresh halibut fillets (6 ounces each)
1	lemon, halved
	Olive oil
	White wine
	Kosher salt

Prepare the salad and divide among four plates. Let them sit at room temperature. Preheat the oven to 500°F. Place the halibut in a baking dish that has been sprayed with nonstick cooking spray, and then squeeze lemon juice on each fillet and let stand for about 5 minutes. Drizzle the olive oil and white wine in equal parts to come about one-third of the way up the side of the fillets. Bake on the lowest rack in the oven until just cooked through, about 12 minutes depending on the thickness. Place one fillet on each salad. Stir all the leftover juices in the pan, and pour them carefully over the halibut and salad. Sprinkle kosher salt to taste on the halibut and serve.

MAKES 4 SERVINGS

DUCK & WONTON SALAD

Philip recommends making Duck and Wonton Salad those days when you are frying anyway and have some type of leftover poultry like duck or pheasant. To feature the duck, simply pan sear a duck breast rare and slice it thinly.

	Boston Lettuce Salad (page 62)
16	*wonton wrappers, about 2 square inches each*
	Canola or vegetable oil
2	*cups pulled duck meat or 16 thin slices rare duck breast*
1	*cup julienned carrots, soaked in ginger ale*

Prepare the salad and divide among four plates without the dressing and reserving the almonds. Heat the oil in a fry pan over high heat. Drop the wonton wrappers in the hot oil and fry for about 15 seconds. Remove to a paper towel. Place 4 hot wontons on each of the salads and ½ cup each of the pulled duck on the wontons. Drain the carrots and arrange on top of each salad. Pour the dressing on top and add the almonds or walnut pieces.

MAKES 4 SERVINGS

ELLOREE CHICKEN SALAD

Ask Philip about his favorite cooking appliance and you will not hear about some mighty Salamander or Viking Range. He likes his tiny Weber Grill in the backyard in Elloree, much preferring it to anything gas-fueled. "After cooking steaks," he says, "I don't want to waste all the energy in the hot coals. So I put a whole chicken on the grill, cover it, and basically don't worry about it until after dessert. When it's cooked through, I put it in the fridge." This makes excellent chicken salad. If you are not grilling, but want chicken salad anyway, you can use a whole poached chicken or an oven-roasted one.

1	whole chicken, charcoal smoked (poached or oven roasted) and pulled into pieces
¼	cup olive oil
2	tablespoons chopped fresh thyme
1	medium Vidalia onion, diced
½	cup finely diced celery
1	tablespoon fresh lemon juice
2	teaspoons kosher salt
2	teaspoons freshly ground black pepper
	Mayonnaise to bind, about ⅓ cup

Put the chicken pieces in a bowl and rub in the olive oil and fresh thyme. Add the onion and celery and mix in the lemon juice. Let stand for about 5 minutes. Add the salt and pepper and bind with the mayonnaise. Refrigerate for at least 1 hour and serve on toasted Kaiser rolls, on grilled bread, or on a salad. In Elloree we just leave the bowl in the refrigerator and have a cup filled with plastic forks. Mysteriously, the contents of the bowl and the forks disappear.

MAKES 4 TO 6 SERVINGS

TOMATO & GOAT CHEESE STACK

Philip recalls, "One of the greatest times of my life was a nervous performance at the James Beard House in New York City. What made it great is I was with Chef Frank Lee of Slightly North of Broad in Charleston. He remains the wisest and closest chef friend I have in a city where all the chefs get along. We have been friends for nearly thirty years. This is the salad we did that night."

8	very ripe red tomato slices, lightly salted
8	ounces goat cheese, cut in 8 (1-ounce) slices
4	very ripe yellow tomato slices, lightly salted
	Olive oil
	Aged balsamic vinegar
	Freshly ground black pepper

Simply place a red tomato slice down and top with a goat cheese slice. Top the goat cheese with a yellow tomato slice, the yellow tomato with a slice of the cheese, and top that with another red tomato slice. Sprinkle with a generous amount of olive oil and balsamic vinegar. Season with the black pepper. (We used Split Farm Creek goat cheese from Anderson, South Carolina, that night. And if you are holding back expensive balsamic vinegar, this is the time to pull it out.)

MAKES 4 SERVINGS

PEANUT, HONEY & BLUE CHEESE SALAD

This salad was inspired by my friends at Coaster's Restaurant in Santee, South Carolina, known for having the best selection of house salads around.

	David's O.P.O. House Salad (page 56)
2	*cups gourmet roasted peanuts*
1	*cup high quality honey*
2	*cups large buttermilk blue cheese crumbles*

Prepare the salad without the pecans or the blue cheese and do not dress the salad yet. Divide the O.P.O. salad among four plates, top with the peanuts, and drizzle the honey carefully over the peanuts to cover as much as possible. Divide the crumbled cheese over the salads, and then top with the O.P.O. House Dressing.

MAKES 4 SERVINGS

BUTTERMILK BLUE CHEESE & CIDER SLAW

Philip describes this recipe as "the Rolls Royce of coleslaw." He advises that if you don't like cabbage, you can use the pre-cut broccoli "slaw" now available in supermarket produce aisles.

4	cups thinly sliced cabbage
1	cup diced Fuji or another sweet, firm apple
¼	cup apple cider vinegar
	Juice of 1 lemon
1	large onion, very thinly sliced
1	cup grated carrot
½	cup buttermilk blue cheese crumbles
1	tablespoon sugar
½	tablespoon kosher salt
2	tablespoons yogurt
	Mayonnaise, optional

Put the cabbage and apple in a mixing bowl and add the cider vinegar. Toss and let stand for 5 minutes. Add the lemon juice, onion, carrot, blue cheese, sugar, salt, and yogurt, and mix gently. Bind ingredients with mayonnaise if desired. If you omit the mayonnaise, you can serve this slaw hot by heating it in a hot, nonstick pan.

MAKES 4 SERVINGS

SAUCES, STOCKS & DRESSINGS

Fruit Reduction Curry Sauce

Marsala Sauce

Blueberry Sauce

Blackjack Sauce

Cold Caper Sauce Maureen

Teriyaki Sauce

Cocktail Sauce

Shrimp Tomato Cream Sauce

Spicy Peanut Sauce

Firecracker Sauce

Jalapeño Tartar Sauce

Hollandaise Sauce

Mousseline Sauce

Mustard Tarragon Sauce

Court-Bouillon

Seafood Stock

Chicken Stock

Duck Stock—Cheatin' Method

O.P.O. House Dressing

Soy Ginger Vinaigrette

Wasabi Vinaigrette

Homemade Mustard

Michel Mix

Aunt Min's Gravy

Country Ham Gravy

Pecan Flour

Seafood Breading

Fritter Batter

Crêpe Batter

FRUIT REDUCTION CURRY SAUCE

While we were finishing renovation of The Old Post Office, I cooked at the popular French restaurant, Mistral, in Charleston, South Carolina," Philip remembers. "The chefs there were young French lads who did not speak English. Despite that, we got along well, and I learned this curry sauce from them."

1	quart (4 cups) chicken stock
2	apples, sliced
3	ripe bananas, peeled and broken into big pieces
2	kiwifruit, peeled and cut in rings
1	orange, peeled and cut in big pieces
2	tablespoons curry powder
1	teaspoon white pepper
1	cinnamon stick
3	tablespoons heavy cream
1	teaspoon cayenne

Bring the stock, apples, bananas, kiwi, orange, curry powder, white pepper, and cinnamon to a boil, and reduce for about 20 minutes, or until most of the liquid is absorbed by the fruit. Strain and discard, reserving the liquid. At this point, the liquid makes an excellent poaching liquid; but to finish the sauce, add the cream and cayenne, and reduce until the desired thickness is achieved. For those who like hot curries, add more cayenne. Serve with grilled chicken and rice.

MAKES 2 CUPS

MARSALA SAUCE

Slightly sweet Marsala is a nice accompaniment for fowl and veal.

4	tablespoons butter
2	pounds cleaned and trimmed mushrooms, thinly sliced
1	shallot, thinly sliced
2	teaspoons dried thyme
1	teaspoon salt
½	cup Marsala
1½	cups Aunt Min's Gravy (page 97) or Country Ham Gravy (page 98)

Melt the butter in a saucepan over high heat until very hot, and add the mushrooms, shallot, thyme, and salt. Cook until the mushrooms brown nicely, and pour in the Marsala. Reduce for about 1 minute and stir in the gravy.

MAKES 2 CUPS

BLUEBERRY SAUCE

An abundance of blueberries grows on Edisto Island, so instead of orange or raspberry sauce, Philip uses blueberry sauce for roast duck.

4	*cups fresh blueberries*
4	*cups freshly squeezed orange juice, or cranberry juice*
2	*tablespoons honey*
2	*tablespoons sugar*

Bring the berries, juice, honey, and sugar to a boil, and simmer until the volume is reduced by one-third. At this point you have two options: You can simply purée the contents, or strain the blueberries (can be saved for something else) and thicken the sauce with a light roux made from duck fat instead of butter.

MAKES 4 CUPS

BLACKJACK SAUCE

This sauce is just a simple infusion of pork medallion marinade and a little cream.

¼	cup duck stock
2	tablespoons molasses
2	tablespoons Jack Daniel's whiskey
2	teaspoons freshly ground black pepper
3	tablespoons heavy cream

Bring the stock, molasses, whiskey, and pepper to a boil in a saucepan and add the cream. Continue to reduce on high heat until the desired thickness is achieved, about 5 minutes. Add more pepper if desired.

MAKES 1 CUP

COLD CAPER SAUCE MAUREEN

Served with smoked fish or any cold meats, this caper sauce is also a great binder for shrimp or chicken salads.

½	cup high quality mayonnaise
¼	cup Dijon mustard
¼	cup sour cream
¼	cup capers, rinsed and chopped
1	shallot, peeled and minced

Blend the mayonnaise, mustard, sour cream, capers, and shallot and chill. Always serve cold.

MAKES ABOUT 1¼ CUPS

TERIYAKI SAUCE

This is easy to make and great to always have on hand. It is particularly good as a last minute addition to sautéed dishes involving rice or as a dip for vegetables.

½   cup fresh ginger, peeled and chopped
1   cup soy sauce
½   cup sherry
     Juice of half an orange

In a food processor, pulse the fresh ginger until it is finely chopped and almost to a mush. Add the soy sauce, sherry and orange juice and pulse for a few minutes longer.

MAKES ABOUT 2 CUPS

COCKTAIL SAUCE

Philip confesses, "When I was at the Loft Oyster Bar in Columbia, South Carolina, I snuck around the corner and lifted some roasted garlic/chili sauce from a nearby Chinese restaurant to add to our cocktail sauce. The blend became so popular that bar customers would order the sauce and crackers as a snack."

2	cups Heinz Chili Sauce (or ketchup)
½	cup prepared horseradish
2	tablespoons oriental chili sauce (Lee Kum Kee Chili/Garlic Sauce)
1	teaspoon Worcestershire sauce
2	teaspoons hot sauce (Frank's Original)
	Juice of 1 lemon

Blend together the chili sauce, horseradish, oriental chili sauce, Worcestershire, hot sauce, and lemon juice. Stir well and chill. This is also an excellent additive to Bloody Marys.

MAKES ABOUT 3 CUPS

Philip Bardin

Aside from the fact that they're delicious, Old Post Office meals are distinguished by their good looks. Well-arranged plates of bright-colored food reveal the sensibilities of a chef with an eye as refined as his tastebuds. Dinner's visual appeal is no surprise when you hear Philip Bardin tell about his experiences as a child when his parents were part of a small colony of artists who spent time on Edisto Island.

He remembers both of his parents by their food preferences. "My mom was a gourmet, a Jackie O type," Philip says. "She would make beef Wellington. My dad was an abstract painter, but he was a country cook. He'd take the Trailways bus to a pond, catch brim, and come home with it rolled in newspaper. I was still crawling around on the floor, but I remember the fish flipping up when he unwrapped them; they were that fresh. He'd cook them up and smoke cigars and the house would smell like crazy."

In addition to what he learned from his parents, Philip found out about food from a black caretaker named Jessie Bell, as well as from his father's family, who ran the old Bardin Hotel in Elloree. In particular he remembers his Aunt Min, whom he describes as "the greatest cook I ever knew. She could make anything: freshwater seafood, any vegetable. When I was in elementary school, she showed me how to do the butterbeans at the hotel."

So began the culinary education of a chef who has become a leading light of Lowcountry cooking. When he graduated high school at a precocious age, sixteen, his stated goal in life was to be a playboy. Teenage dreams aside, gastronomy was part of his character, and his first paying job was in concession sales at a community theater. Shortly after that, he became a busboy in a Charleston restaurant. "At the restaurant I kept getting kicked upstairs," he recalls. "The chefs taught me all the basics and the classical European dishes, and I married what

I learned from them with what I had gotten as a child from my family. It was a seat-of-the-pants education, and I found myself on a fast track. You see, most of the chefs were mean drunks who kept getting fired. Every time that happened, I'd fill in. When I was twenty, I had become head chef at the Loft Oyster Bar in Columbia."

Philip recalls that grouper was then a little-known dish beyond the community of fishermen who caught it. But he began serving it as part of a menu of South Carolina seafood—a career move that put it on the culinary map to such a degree that it has become scarce. "I regret that," he says. "If it hadn't been for me and Steve Jackson, all those fish would still be swimming in the ocean."

In 1983 Philip suffered through a one-hundred-degree heat wave in Columbia, where he was supervising the kitchens of three different Loft restaurants. It was after that he decided he couldn't stand the heat. So he got out of the Loft kitchen and moved to a resort kitchen in the ocean-breeze-swept community of Edisto.

Philip was no stranger to the island, having traveled there many summers with his family. He says, "There has always been a strong connection between New York City and Edisto. Mostly it is because of Jasper Johns, who came down here all the time. I think his presence encouraged other artists to come; and my parents were part of that community. I remember when I first met him. I was a child. We had caught a mouse in the house. I didn't know what to do with it. JAP, as we called him, came over and took it out for me."

It was shortly after he moved to Edisto that Philip happened to discover that one of his neighbors was David Gressette, whom he had known for a short while when both of them were growing up in Columbia. Philip recalled his own childhood food memories and David remembered the glorious fish dinners on his own family's table. Years ago, a restaurant called Tatum Gressette's Place was a popular beachside destination for residents and vacationing visitors. With a little encouragement from friends, the two men decided to open a restaurant together.

"Our first menu was shrimp fettuccine and about three other things," Philip says. It wasn't much, and there were many people who predicted we didn't have a chance in hell to survive. But there was no other place to go on the island for a nice meal. People came from around here, and they drove to Edisto from small towns on the mainland because it was either here or a trip all the way into Charleston."

To explain the special appeal of what he serves, Philip demurs at boasting of his own prodigious talent. Instead, he attributes its goodness to the local ambience, quite literally. "I believe my food tastes better because so much of it is from Edisto, where everything is aromaticized by salt air," he explains. "We have it all here on the island. The fertile soil and ocean breezes make our produce the best." Today's menu is, of course, far broader than three entrees. It is a dramatic tutorial in coastal cookery, from Edisto clam chowder through fried oysters and stuffed shrimp to firecracker flounder and the famous oyster skillet. And always, great vegetables and grits on the side.

SHRIMP TOMATO CREAM SAUCE

You will need the reserved liquid from the Shrimp Pâte recipe (page 14); or cook a dozen small shrimp in white wine and a little Firecracker Sauce and purée them.

½	*cup pâte liquid reserve*
½	*cup heavy cream (always use 40%)*

Boil the pâte liquid and heavy cream, and reduce until thick, about 5 minutes.

MAKES ABOUT 1 CUP

Note: This is an excellent sauce for blackened or grilled fish.

SPICY PEANUT SAUCE

This sauce is good for ribs or shish kabobs with grilled plantains.

1	*cup heavy cream*
2	*tablespoons smooth peanut butter*
2	*teaspoons cayenne*
	Salt

In a small saucepan over high heat, bring the cream to a boil, stir in the peanut butter and the cayenne, and stir until thick, just a few minutes. Depending on your choice of peanut butter, salt may or may not need to be added.

MAKES ABOUT 1 CUP

FIRECRACKER SAUCE

The O.P.O. has put Firecracker Sauce on fried flounder since the first year they opened. It is a favorite among those who prefer the hotter things in life.

1	*red sweet pepper, thinly sliced*
1	*green bell pepper, thinly sliced*
4	*small jalapeños, cut in rings or seeded and minced*
2	*firecracker peppers (difficult to find: substitute 4 Tabasco peppers), diced*
1	*medium onion, thinly sliced*
2	*tablespoons olive oil*
1	*tablespoon chopped fresh thyme leaves*
2	*teaspoons dried oregano*
3	*cups tomato sauce or puréed tomatoes*
1	*cup Bloody Mary mix (Zing Zang)*
¼	*cup hot sauce (Frank's Original)*
1	*tablespoon sugar*
2	*teaspoons salt*

In a medium pot sauté all of the peppers and the onion in the olive oil over high heat, and add the thyme and oregano. Continue to cook on high heat, stirring until the ingredients brown somewhat, about 5 minutes. Add the tomatoes, Bloody Mary mix, hot sauce, sugar, and salt. Simmer on low heat for about 20 minutes.

MAKES 5 CUPS

JALAPEÑO TARTAR SAUCE

O.P.O. house tartar sauce appeals to that huge contingency of Edistonians who love spicy foods.

1	cup mayonnaise
1	tablespoon lemon juice
1	tablespoon Dijon mustard
1	shallot, minced
2	medium jalapeño peppers, seeded and minced
1	tablespoon sweet pickle relish
1	teaspoon white pepper
1	teaspoon salt

In a mixing bowl blend the mayonnaise, lemon juice, mustard, shallot, peppers, relish, white pepper, and salt. Refrigerate for at least 1 day.

MAKES ABOUT 1½ CUPS

Ocean breezes waft over Edisto, perfuming the air and, according to Chef Philip Bardin, adding inimitable zest to all the island's foods.

When this was the site of Edisto's post office, it was a gathering place for locals. Now that it is a restaurant, it still is ... and the trappings of the Old Post Office remain. Below are the original mailboxes.

*Philip Bardin in the kitchen of
The Old Post Office Restaurant.*

*Philip demonstrates how to
squeeze a lemon so that the juices
run down your thumb and drip
exactly where you want them.*

Down a long dirt road and nearly overgrown with foliage, George & Pink vegetable stand is an opportunity to browse among some of the extraordinary produce that is grown in Edisto soil.

Shrimp & Grits (page 139)

Oyster Skillet (page 127)

Cracklin' Roast Duck Ltd. (page 185)

Firecracker Flounder (page 158)

Key Lime Pie (page 205)

Coca Cola Cake (page 201)

HOLLANDAISE SAUCE

Egg phobia of recent years means that few people make hollandaise sauce from scratch any more. The use of pasteurized egg yolks will alleviate fears.

4	*egg yolks*
2	*teaspoons lemon juice*
¼	*pound butter, melted and boiling hot (use Plugra butter)*
	Dash of cayenne
1	*teaspoon salt*

Put the egg yolks and lemon juice in a blender and add the butter in a slow steady stream; make sure the butter is very hot. Blend in the cayenne and salt.

MAKES ABOUT 1 CUP

Variation: Maltaise Sauce is an absolutely delicious, but rarely seen, sauce. Make the hollandaise sauce recipe above, but substitute 1 tablespoon freshly squeezed orange juice for the lemon juice. It's a change for any recipe that uses hollandaise and especially good on grilled fish and poached eggs with ham.

MOUSSELINE SAUCE

One of the most luxurious dishes on The Old Post Office menu—on any menu, anywhere—is shrimp over creamy grits blanketed with mousseline sauce.

4	*egg yolks*
2	*teaspoons lemon juice*
¼	*pound butter, melted and boiling hot (use Plugra butter)*
	Dash of cayenne
1	*teaspoon salt*
2	*tablespoons heavy cream*

Put the egg yolks and lemon juice in a blender and add the butter in a slow steady stream; make sure the butter is very hot. Blend in the cayenne and salt. Add 2 tablespoons heavy cream. If you wish to have the sauce thicker, place a bowl over a pot of softly boiling water, and stir constantly with a whisk until thick.

MAKES ABOUT 1 CUP

MUSTARD TARRAGON SAUCE

The aromatic anise zest of tarragon and the punch of Dijon mustard make this one of the brightest sauces, especially welcome on such sturdy slabs of fish as salmon or swordfish.

4	*egg yolks*
2	*tablespoons Dijon mustard*
2	*teaspoons lemon juice*
¼	*pound butter, melted and boiling hot (use Plugra butter)*
2	*tablespoons chopped fresh tarragon*
	Dash of cayenne
1	*teaspoon salt*
2	*tablespoons heavy cream*

Put the egg yolks, mustard, and lemon juice in a blender and add the butter in a slow steady stream; make sure the butter is very hot. Blend in the tarragon, cayenne, and salt. Add 2 tablespoons heavy cream. If you wish to have the sauce thicker, place a bowl over a pot of softly boiling water, and stir constantly with a whisk until thick.

MAKES ABOUT 1 CUP

COURT-BOUILLON

Poaching is an under-employed cooking technique nowadays, and Philip notes that court-bouillon, the liquid used for poaching, is seldom seen or heard of. "When I was coming up in the old days," he says, "it was very essential . . . and essential it be done right. Once one graduated from cold preparations and was allowed on the stove, it was the first thing taught. Its uses are many, but its primary purpose is poaching seafood."

2	quarts (8 cups) water (you can also use fish stock)
¼	cup champagne vinegar
½	cup tarragon vinegar
1	bay leaf
1	medium carrot, roughly chopped
1	small onion, peeled and halved, with 4 cloves stuck inside
1	lemon, cut in half
2	sprigs parsley
2	sprigs oregano
2	sprigs thyme
2	teaspoons salt

Put the water, vinegars, bay leaf, carrot, onion, lemon, parsley, oregano, thyme, and salt in a saucepan. Bring to a boil for about 1 minute and simmer for another 5 minutes. Remove the bay leaf. Cover and let stand for 1 hour. Strain the liquid. It is ready to use or to save for later.

MAKES ABOUT 8 CUPS

SEAFOOD STOCK

It is commonly believed that the longer you reduce a stock, the better it will be. That is not the case with fish stocks, since they can become too strong, especially if the fish head, bones, and tail are not cleaned thoroughly.

2	*pounds cleaned (snapper or grouper) fish heads, bones, and tail (or Dover sole backbones if you can get them)*
1	*quart (4 cups) water*
1	*pint (2 cups) Court-Bouillon (page 88)*
1	*large onion, sliced*
1	*carrot, roughly chopped*
1	*rib celery, cut in big pieces*
1	*stem each parsley and thyme*
1	*teaspoon salt*

Put the fish bones in a big pot with the cold water and court-bouillon. Bring to a boil over high heat, and add the rest of the ingredients. When the boiling point returns, slow to a simmer for about 20 to 30 minutes, skimming the top occasionally. Remove from the heat and strain through a fine sieve or cheesecloth. Let stand for 1 hour and then either use or refrigerate.

MAKES ABOUT 4 CUPS

CHICKEN STOCK

One of the great things about this recipe is that aside from making chicken stock, you also wind up with a whole cooked chicken to use.

1	whole chicken, about 3 pounds, with excess fat removed
3	quarts (12 cups) water
1	tablespoon kosher salt
6	black peppercorns
1	carrot, cut in thick slices
1	onion, peeled and quartered
1	sprig thyme (1 teaspoon dried)
1	sprig rosemary (1 teaspoon dried)
1	small bunch parsley
2	teaspoons turmeric
1	tablespoon Worcestershire sauce

In a large stockpot over high heat bring the chicken, water, salt, peppercorns, carrot, onion, thyme, rosemary, parsley, turmeric, and Worcestershire to a boil. Turn heat to low, cover, and simmer until the chicken is cooked through, about 30 to 45 minutes. Carefully remove the chicken, and let cool on a plate while the stockpot is off the heat. Pick all the meat off the chicken, and save for another dish (chicken crepes, salad, etc.). Cut the carcass in half, and return it with all the juices left on the plate to the stock. Return the stockpot to a slow simmer—this time uncovered—for about 1 hour. Strain, cool, and refrigerate the stock. The following day remove the fat from the top. It is now ready to use or freeze.

MAKES ABOUT 8 CUPS

DUCK STOCK—CHEATIN' METHOD

The duck stock used at The Old Post Office does not involve long and laborious traditional stock reductions. "I get away with it," Philip says, "because I roast ducks every day. But you can do it when preparing my Cracklin' Roast Duck. The wine and seasonings from the duck pan are all you need."

Liquid from Cracklin' Roast Duck recipe (page 185)

After following the duck recipe, take all of the liquid and put in a medium-size, clear plastic container. Cool and refrigerate for at least 24 hours. The following day, if it is chilled properly, you will have somewhat of an aspic. Take the fat off and reserve in another container. The rest of the "glace" remains, but you will see where all the sediment has settled at the bottom (about one-tenth of the total volume). Remove and discard. What is left is a perfectly rich and delicious duck stock you can either use as is or reduce more.

Note: Perfectly rendered duck fat is ideal for roux, piecrusts, and is my secret weapon for collard greens. It has great flavor and is lower in cholesterol than butter. Using the saved fat from the duck-stock method, melt the bright white fat, and if any specks of brown appear, skim them away. Bring to a high heat, cool, and refrigerate for future use. (For the adventuresome cook, you can use this purification process as an excuse to fry something in the duck fat—such as French fries. I have also secretively done shrimp, a task, I promise you, that is outstanding.)

O.P.O. HOUSE DRESSING

Philip created the recipe for house dressing when he was barely eighteen years old. By now, he's blasé about it. "But customers have been asking me to fill wine bottles with it for them to take home since its inception," he says. "Despite my lack of enthusiasm, it does make a dandy marinade, and it has a host of other uses."

3	cups Dijon mustard
3	tablespoons honey
1	cup red wine vinegar
3	cups salad oil
1	tablespoon Dutch poppy seeds

Put the mustard in a chilled bowl. Whisking rapidly and constantly, add the honey, vinegar and—in a slow steady stream—the oil. It has never happened to me, but some folks have reported not getting a smooth result from this. For those rare individuals, use a blender or food processor. Stir in the poppy seeds at the end.

MAKES 6 CUPS

SOY GINGER VINAIGRETTE

I once saw Martha Stewart place a few knobs of ginger in soy sauce to flavor the sauce," Philip recalls. "Like a lot of tricks I have learned from her, I tinkered with the idea and came up with this." This is outstanding on watercress with grilled fish or as an all-purpose dressing or marinade.

2	big pieces peeled, fresh ginger (about 1 ounce each)
½	cup soy sauce
½	cup freshly squeezed orange juice
1	sprig rosemary
½	cup Dijon mustard
3	tablespoons balsamic vinegar
1	cup olive oil

Soak the ginger in the soy sauce, orange juice, and rosemary. After about 1 hour, discard the rosemary, and finely mince the ginger with a very sharp knife. Return the ginger to the mixture. Put the mustard in a mixing bowl, whisk in the orange juice mixture and vinegar, and slowly stir in the olive oil.

MAKES 3 CUPS

WASABI VINAIGRETTE

Over the years, I have played host to many excellent sous chefs," Philip says. "One was Iowa native Bill Twaler, now chef at his own restaurant in Hollywood, South Carolina, the Old Firehouse. Bill has a knack for ingenious, fast preparations. He came up with this vinaigrette and it remains with me."

½ cup wasabi powder
½ cup cold water
1 cup O.P.O. House Dressing (page 92)

Blend the wasabi powder with the cold water. Then whisk in the house dressing. Put the mixture in a squeeze bottle and refrigerate. This stuff is good on just about anything.

MAKES ABOUT 2 CUPS

HOMEMADE MUSTARD

This is a great accompaniment for roasted meats or fried duck livers.

½	cup dry English mustard
½	cup cold water
¼	cup honey
1	teaspoon tarragon vinegar

Mix the mustard and cold water very well. Blend in the honey and vinegar. Chill until ready for use. For best flavor, serve at room temperature.

MAKES 1 CUP

MICHEL MIX

This is an essential ingredient in many Old Post Office recipes. When the great French chef Michel Guerard was at the peak of his popularity with his "Cuisine Minceur," Philip learned to place fresh blends like these rather than heavy sauces on grilled beef, poultry, and fish.

1	*medium bulb garlic, all cloves peeled*
3	*shallots, peeled and cut in half*
1	*large bunch parsley, washed, with most of the stems removed*
1	*tablespoon kosher salt*
1	*tablespoon olive oil*

Using the pulse mode, chop the garlic, shallots, and parsley with the salt with the steel blade of a food processor. You can also mince this finely with a good knife. Do not over process. Stir in the olive oil and reserve for use.

MAKES ABOUT 1½ CUPS

AUNT MIN'S GRAVY

When the old Bardin Hotel in Elloree still stood and was home to my family, great cuisine flourished," Philip reminisces. "My late Aunt Minnie Lee Blackman was hands-down the best cook in town, and I was lucky to spend many summer days over the years at her stove and at her apron strings. She could take something someone else cooked, stir it once with her spoon, and it would be miraculously improved (as was my life each day I saw her)."

4	cups duck stock (page 91)
4	tablespoons butter
4	tablespoons flour
2	tablespoons heavy cream
	Freshly ground black pepper

Heat the duck stock in a saucepan over medium heat. In a separate pot melt the butter over medium-high heat. Make a roux by whisking in the flour and cooking over medium heat until nice and smooth, about 3 minutes. Whisk the roux into the hot duck stock and add the heavy cream. Give a few grindings of black pepper if desired. This is an excellent, all-purpose gravy.

MAKES 4½ CUPS

COUNTRY HAM GRAVY

Ham gravy is made for stuffed pork tenderloin, but it also works splendidly on open-faced sandwiches, rice, roast rabbit, or roast pork.

1	*small onion, minced*
½	*cup country ham, cut into small pieces*
1	*tablespoon butter*
2	*cups Aunt Min's Gravy (page 97)*

Sauté the onion and country ham in the butter in a medium saucepan over medium-high heat until the onion is translucent and the ham is browned. Add the gravy, stirring in with a whisk to get everything clinging to the bottom.

MAKES 2½ CUPS

PECAN FLOUR

O.P.O. pecans come from the Golden Kernel Pecan Company in Cameron, South Carolina. Pecan flour is used for coating chicken, quail, and veal.

2	*cups pecan pieces*
2	*cups hi-gluten flour*
1	*tablespoon salt*

In a food processor pulse the pecans, flour, and salt, making sure to leave some of the pecan pieces visible. Store in a plastic bag in a dry, cool place.

MAKES 4 CUPS

SEAFOOD BREADING

Philip advises keeping seafood breading on hand so whenever you get a good piece of fish or shellfish, you are ready to fry it.

3	cups hi-gluten bread flour
1	cup cracker meal, fine or medium grind (we use Lance)
¼	cup Old Bay Seasoning
1	tablespoon salt
1	tablespoon pepper

Mix the flour, meal, Old Bay, salt, and pepper together well, and you are ready to go.

MAKES ABOUT 4 CUPS

FRITTER BATTER

Fritters are usually too spongy and concealing, but this recipe turns out nicely. I prefer it with banana peppers, but it also works fine for those liking seafood fritters.

1½	cups all-purpose flour
1	teaspoon salt
1	teaspoon white pepper
1	teaspoon ground ginger
1	tablespoon safflower oil
2	egg yolks, beaten
¾	cup beer, at room temperature

Blend in a mixing bowl the flour, salt, pepper, ginger, oil, and egg yolks. Add the beer, stirring constantly. Refrigerate the batter for at least 3 hours before using. I like to add a beaten egg white or two and fold this in at the last minute.

MAKES 2 CUPS

CRÊPE BATTER

Crêpes have taken the same unfortunate road as the great quiches and are rarely seen (and almost never made from scratch anymore)," Philip laments. "This batter is for main course, not dessert, crêpes."

6	*eggs*
¼	*teaspoon salt*
2	*tablespoons water*
¼	*cup all-purpose flour, sifted*

Beat the eggs thoroughly with the water. Gradually add the flour until smooth. Use a ladle to pour about ¾ cup batter into a hot crêpe pan. Swirl the batter and flip when bubbles start to form. This should make perfect 6-inch crêpes, which are now easily done with advance technology in nonstick pans. I still prefer to ladle the batter in a rolled steel pan with plenty of hot oil.

MAKES 10 (6-INCH) CRÊPES

· SIDE DISHES ·

FIRST CLASS

Rice
Risotto with Lemon & Goat Cheese
Oyster Stuffing
O.P.O. Grits
Mashed Yukon Gold Potatoes
Rosemary Roasted Potatoes
Potatoes Anna
Sweet Corn Dumplings
Cassina Point Asparagus
Collard Greens
Butter Beans
Vegetables Fleetwood
Zucchini Crust
Fried Okra
Fried Banana Peppers
Boiled Peanuts

RICE

It used to be said that the test of a Lowcountry cook was how well the cook made Okra Soup. Philip, on the other hand, believes that rice is the benchmark. He says that because Lowcountry food is historically the food of the long-gone rice plantations, local rice can be hard to get. "That is why, much to the surprise of many, I almost always use Arborio rice."

1	*medium onion, finely chopped*
1	*tablespoon butter*
1	*teaspoon olive oil*
1	*cup Arborio rice*
2	*cups hot chicken stock*
2	*teaspoons salt*

Sauté the onion in the butter and olive oil on medium heat in a saucepot that has a tight fitting lid. When the onion is tender, add the rice, and stir until all the grains are coated. Add 1 cup stock, bringing it to a furious boil and stirring constantly. Add the second cup of stock and the salt, and stir well after a good boil is present. Reduce to a low simmer, cover for about 15 minutes, and remove from the heat. After 5 minutes fluff with a fork and serve.

MAKES 4 SERVINGS

RISOTTO WITH LEMON & GOAT CHEESE

This dish was developed by O.P.O. Chef Bethany Fill and offers a great twist to plain risotto.

1	*recipe Rice (page 105)*
2	*tablespoons fresh thyme leaves*
3	*ounces softened goat cheese, crumbled*
2	*tablespoons freshly squeezed lemon juice*

Prepare the rice recipe, but prior to covering stir the thyme, goat cheese, and lemon juice into the prepared rice, and leave the pan uncovered for several extra minutes before covering. Cook for about 15 minutes and remove from the heat. After 5 minutes fluff with a fork and serve.

This dish is outstanding with lamb.

MAKES 4 SERVINGS

OYSTER STUFFING

Oyster stuffing makes its way to our menu in the fall. We often use it to stuff pork tenderloin, and it is outstanding on its own.

1	*medium onion, finely sliced*
1	*stalk celery, finely sliced*
1	*tablespoon butter*
1	*pint freshly shucked oysters in their liquor*
½	*cup heavy cream or seafood stock*
3	*cups cubed O.P.O. Bread (page 35) or French bread*
2	*teaspoons dried sage*
2	*teaspoons dried thyme*
1	*teaspoon white pepper*

In a medium pan on low heat sauté the onion and celery in the butter until tender. Add the oysters with the cream or (for a lighter version) the stock. Bring up the heat until the mixture is just warm. Put the bread cubes in a mixing bowl and pour in the oyster mixture. Add the sage, thyme, and white pepper. Check for salt because this dish is completely influenced by the integrity of your oysters. This can be baked in a baking dish or used for a stuffing. If you want to get really fancy with the ever-popular deep-fried turkey, triple this recipe, and stuff the bird first for a blissful overkill.

MAKES 4 SERVINGS

Variation: For country ham stuffing follow the exact recipe above, except omit the oysters and substitute ½ cup country ham pieces and 1½ cups good, regular coffee. This is used for stuffing pork tenderloin or quail.

O.P.O. GRITS

For years, we took it on the chin for serving grits at night," Philip reports. "Now it seems to be done everywhere. We have ours specially ground for us and bagged under The Old Post Office label. If you use a coarser brand, I suggest using a stick-free pot."

1	cup water
1	cup milk
1	cup heavy cream
1	cup melted butter
1	teaspoon salt
1	cup whole-grain grits
1	cup grated sharp Cheddar cheese

Bring the water, milk, cream, butter, and salt to a low boil. Add the grits, stirring rapidly on medium heat. Stir and watch for 20 minutes, being careful not to let the grits stick. Stir in the cheese, pour the grits into a crock-pot or a double boiler, and continue cooking for at least 1 hour.

MAKES 4 SERVINGS

Variation: The classic ratio is four parts liquid to one part grits. Sometimes I like to cook grits in duck stock if they are accompanying roasted quail for example. Grits cooked in half water and half thin red-eye gravy is a spectacular surprise at breakfast.

Grits

In the Lowcountry, grits are frequently listed on menus as "creamy grits." The adjective is not kitchen propaganda. South Carolina's creamy grits are dramatically different from the watery white ones that accompany breakfast in countless diners throughout the region. They are slow-cooked for a minimum of one hour, sometimes nearly all day, during which time they absorb maximum amounts of butter and milk or cream. The result is a compelling paradox: rugged maize that's custard-lush.

Alongside a pillow of brittle-crusted fried flounder or blanketed with a spill of firm, broiled shrimp, they are grain transcendent.

Excellent grits are such an important part of the local cookery that The Old Post Office sets each table in the dining room not only with salt and pepper, but also with a one-pound bag of them, uncooked of course. Because the grits sold in supermarkets tend to be the bleached-pale, tasteless variety, customers who are cooks buy The Old Post Office bags to take home and prepare for themselves. Here in the restaurant, creamy grits are part of nearly every meal served, either as a side dish on a plate with butter beans, or as the bottom layer of a meal, forming a luxurious cushion across which are strewn a school of spicy shrimp and mousseline.

"Most chefs do their stocks first thing in the morning," Philip Bardin told us one day at 9 A.M. as he whisked two pounds of the ground-to-order grain into a pot of butter-yellow liquid on the stove. "Here, we start the day with grits. I do them early and keep them on the steam table for hours, the longer the better."

MASHED YUKON GOLD POTATOES

Yukon Golds were originally touted because they had a buttery, salty flavor without adding too much butter or salt. Philip says he likes them because of their thin skins and sweetness, noting they can be mashed with very little butter or milk if you boil them in chicken stock.

6	*medium Yukon Gold potatoes, scrubbed and cut in half*
4	*cups chicken stock*
1	*teaspoon salt*
	Melted butter
	Cream or milk

Put the potatoes in a large pot, and bring to a boil over high heat. Reduce the heat, cover, and simmer for 20 to 30 minutes until potatoes stick easily with a fork. Drain away half the stock, and mash the potatoes with a heavy whip or old-fashioned potato masher (I like to put the pot on a sturdy table). Add melted butter and cream to the desired consistency and check for salt.

MAKES 6 SERVINGS

ROSEMARY ROASTED POTATOES

This simple dish has a marvelous aroma when removed from the oven. The flavor does not disappoint.

4	cups washed and quartered new or red bliss potatoes
1	tablespoon salt
2	tablespoons herbes de Provence
3	tablespoons olive oil

Preheat the oven to 350°F. In a mixing bowl gently stir together the potatoes, salt, herbs, and olive oil so the potatoes are well coated. Spread out evenly on a baking sheet and toast for about 20 minutes. If they are overcooked, they are crunchy and delicious—better than most French fries. You can also chill these and add some sun-dried tomatoes and a dressing of your choice for an unusually good potato salad.

MAKES 4 SERVINGS

POTATOES ANNA

Philip was playing around with scallops and potatoes and named this "scalloped potato dish" for his friend Ann Burger, former food editor of the *Charleston Post & Courier.*

6	*new potatoes*
6	*medium sea scallops*
1	*tablespoon butter*
1	*teaspoon salt*
1	*teaspoon pepper*
3	*tablespoons heavy cream*
2	*tablespoons Parmesan cheese*

Peel and cut the ends off the potatoes. Carefully hollow them out, and poach them in chicken stock until just done, about 10 minutes. In a saucepan melt the butter, sauté the fresh sea scallops until about halfway cooked (just a few minutes), and add the salt, pepper, and heavy cream. Reduce on high heat and stir in the Parmesan cheese. When this pan reduction is thick enough to coat the back of a spoon, remove from the heat. On a plate arrange the potatoes, and place 1 scallop on each potato. Pour the sauce over the arrangement. Freshly snipped chives make an appropriate finishing touch.

MAKES 2 SERVINGS

SWEET CORN DUMPLINGS

What makes this special is the nectar of the fresh sweet corn. And while it makes a great accompaniment, it also stands well as a simple main dish.

4	*cups chicken stock*
1	*medium onion, minced*
2	*cups sweet corn, cut fresh off the cob with juices*
1	*teaspoon salt*
1	*teaspoon black pepper*
1	*teaspoon lemon juice*
1	*cup raw biscuit dough (or store-bought dumplings work well)*

Bring the stock, onion, corn, salt, pepper, and lemon juice to a boil. Let simmer on low for 10 minutes. Break the biscuit dough into pieces, and cook on low for another 5 to 10 minutes. Thicken with a little cornstarch and water (about 1 tablespoon each) mixture if desired. Let stand 5 minutes before serving. Check for salt.

MAKES 6 SERVINGS

Note: I like a little extra lemon in mine, and one other good tip: Use sweet potato biscuit dough (page 39) for an interesting and delicious taste.

CASSINA POINT ASPARAGUS

For years a delicately thin asparagus is grown at Cassina Point Plantation on Edisto by the seaside. It was notable by its almost blue color. Select thin spring asparagus stalks for a dish that replicates that old plantation dish.

2	*dozen asparagus with ends trimmed off evenly*
1	*tablespoon Michel Mix (page 96)*
1	*teaspoon kosher salt*
2	*tablespoons sherry vinegar*
4	*tablespoons high quality olive oil*

Blanch the asparagus in salted boiling water until just tender, just a few minutes, depending on thinness. Plunge in ice water, drain, and keep the asparagus chilled.

Combine the mix, salt, vinegar, and olive oil, and pour over the asparagus. I like to sauce chilled plates with the vinaigrette, fan out the asparagus, and garnish with jumbo lump crabmeat.

MAKES 4 SERVINGS

COLLARD GREENS

Philip says the secret weapon in cooking collard greens is duck fat. "Children, or even adults repulsed at the idea of Southern-style greens, will often change their minds if the greens are prepared in this manner." He also advises that although collards can now be found year round, they are still best picked out of the field after a frost.

3	quarts (12 cups) chicken stock
1	smoked ham hock
1	cup rendered duck fat
2	tablespoons brown sugar
1	bunch collard greens (about 4 pounds), washed and torn into large pieces without the ribs and stalk

Bring the stock, ham hock, duck fat, and brown sugar to a boil for 20 to 30 minutes. Take off the heat and let stand for 1 hour. Return to a boil, add the collard greens, and cook until tender, lowering the heat and simmering for 1 hour. Cover, remove from the heat, and let stand for another 30 minutes.

MAKES 8 SERVINGS

Note: If collards are not tender enough, you can cook them longer. Some folks enjoy a shot of pepper vinegar or Tabasco sauce to finish. Strained, leftover, cold collards make an excellent egg-roll or spring-roll filling.

BUTTER BEANS

 M y first kitchen job as a child was shelling butter beans," Philip recalls. "The pain of green fibers under a thumbnail is a feeling I won't forget. Nevertheless, they are delicious. I am partial to the large Fordhook beans."

3	quarts (12 cups) chicken stock
1	medium onion, diced
1	smoked ham hock
2	pounds Fordhook beans or lima beans, fresh or frozen

In a large stockpot, bring the stock, onion, and ham hock to a boil over high heat. Add the beans and simmer for 30 to 40 minutes until tender.

MAKES 8 SERVINGS

VEGETABLES FLEETWOOD

Vegetables Fleetwood was named for a vegan patron of the Loft Oyster Bar who appreciated the fact that all vegetables there were steamed to order.

4	*broccoli spears*
4	*cauliflower pieces*
4	*baby carrots, peeled, and tops removed*
6	*fresh Brussels sprouts*
1	*red bell pepper, quartered*
	Jane's Crazy Mixed-Up Salt (seasoned salt)
	Juice of 1 lemon

Arrange the broccoli, cauliflower, carrots, Brussels sprouts, and bell pepper in an oval casserole dish that will fit in any steaming pot or vessel you can provide. Sprinkle the vegetables liberally with the salt (if you cannot find Jane's, kosher salt and various vegetable salts will work). Steam for about 10 minutes or until desired tenderness is achieved. Remove the casserole carefully, and serve immediately with a splash of lemon juice. This can be a beautiful dish, so be imaginative in the arranging. I liked to serve it with Maltaise Sauce (variation on page 85).

MAKES 4 SERVINGS

ZUCCHINI CRUST

If you are looking for a substitute for flour-based pizza crust, try making one with zucchini. You can top it with other things or serve it on its own.

2	large zucchini, grated and patted dry with paper towels
1	cup grated mozzarella cheese
1	tablespoon whole-wheat flour

Preheat the oven to 425°F. Mix the zucchini, cheese, and flour. Mash and form the mix into circles large or small. Bake until crisp. You can top the crust with tomato sauce and cheese (even pepperoni), or leave it as it is with a drizzle of olive oil.

MAKES 4 SERVINGS

FRIED OKRA

Fried okra is a hallmark dish of the South. At The Old Post Office they fry whole baby okra, but the more traditional way is to cut the okra into rings as follows.

	Vegetable oil for frying
2	*cups freshly cut okra rings*
2	*cups buttermilk*
	Seafood Breading (page 100) with some cornmeal added (if desired)

Fill a skillet with 2 inches of oil and heat on medium-high to 350°F. Soak the okra in the buttermilk while oil is heating. Drain the okra from the buttermilk and dredge through the breading. Fry in the hot oil until golden brown, just a few minutes. If you want to do the whole baby pods, follow the same recipe but just fry the pods longer, about 3 minutes.

MAKES 4 SERVINGS

FRIED BANANA PEPPERS

Sweet banana peppers grow abundantly in the Lowcountry, but they are even more popular in Bluegrass Country, where the late Elloree native and great jockey, Chris Antley, won the Kentucky Derby twice.

1½	cups fritter batter
6	large banana peppers, split and seeded
	Vegetable oil for frying
	Salt and pepper

Dip the banana peppers in the fritter batter. In a large skillet heat the oil to 350°F and fry the peppers, turning once. Cook each side about 1 minute. Drain on paper towels and sprinkle with salt and pepper.

MAKES 4 SERVINGS

BOILED PEANUTS

Philip's cousin, Lee Bardin Blackman Jr. is the proprietor of Bardin Farms in Elloree, South Carolina, where, he says, the best Spanish peanuts are to be found. "I have made boiled peanuts in many ways, but here is my favorite."

4	pounds fresh green Spanish peanuts in the shell (the largest you can find)
4	tablespoons salt
4	quarts (16 cups) water
½	cup white balsamic or champagne vinegar

In a large stockpot over high heat add the peanuts, salt, water, and vinegar. Boil the peanuts, uncovered, for about 1½ hours. Remove from the heat, and let stand in a cool place for another 1½ hours.

MAKES 12 SERVINGS

·SEAFOOD·

Jambalaya

Oyster Pie

Oyster Skillet

My Angel's Crab & Asparagus Pie

O.P.O. Crab Cakes

Stone Crab Claws & Shrimp

Shrimp with Feta, Capers & Ouzo

Shrimp in Grand Marnier Sauce

Fresh Shrimp with Creamy Pasta

Shrimp Creole

Shrimp & Grits

Rare Grilled Sea Scallops

Seafood Crêpes

"Needs Help" Grilled Tuna

Tuna for Salad

Salmon with Spinach Mousse & Maltaise Sauce

Steamed Bowl of Mussels

Embrace of Grouper & Soft-Shell Crab

Cayenne & Honey-Sizzled Catfish

Min's Freshwater Fish with Cucumbers & Dill

William's Wellington

Whole Steamed Porgy

Grilled Dolphin with Red Bliss Potatoes & Watercress

Flounder & Shrimp Bake

A-1 Wahoo

Firecracker Flounder

Flounder Michel

Dolphin "Miss Pink"

Pan-Roasted Bluefish with Red Wine & Capers

JAMBALAYA

Jambalaya takes many forms, from Louisiana jambalaya to similar dishes throughout the old Lowcountry plantations that offer something similar. The name alone terrifies me as I first prepared it professionally at the tender age of twenty for a lovely woman named Anne-Marie who turned out to be Jacqueline Kennedy's chef.

1	tablespoon olive oil
1	tablespoon butter
½	cup country ham cubes
1	dozen shrimp, peeled and deveined
½	cup cooked onion sausage or spicy sausage
1	medium onion, thinly sliced
1	medium bell pepper, thinly sliced
1	garlic clove, thinly sliced
1	tablespoon Cajun seasoning
1	cup freshly made tomato sauce (or canned)
2	teaspoons sugar
2	cups cooked rice

Bring the olive oil and butter to a high heat in a heavy pot. Add the ham, shrimp, sausage, onion, bell pepper, garlic, and seasoning to the pot. Sauté the ingredients quickly, and as soon as the shrimp are almost done, stir in the tomato sauce and sugar. Lower the heat to a simmer. Stir in the rice, remove from the heat, and cover. Let stand for a few minutes before serving. Freshly ground black pepper to finish is a good option.

MAKES 4 SERVINGS

OYSTER PIE

When I was very young, oyster pie consisted of oysters, saltines, and sherry," Philip recalls. "Now that crackers are no longer made with animal fat, the old recipes are not as good. But this adjusted recipe works well."

1	pint oysters
1	cup Ritz crackers, broken into pieces
½	cup breadcrumbs
5	tablespoons butter, cut in small pats
1	tablespoon sherry
¼	cup half-and-half

Preheat the oven to 425°F. Coat a baking dish well with nonstick spray. Combine the cracker crumbs and breadcrumbs. Put a layer of the crumb mix on the bottom of the dish. Drain the oysters, saving the liquor, and layer them on the crumb mix. Dot the oysters with the butter pats. Repeat the layering, ending with the crumb mixture with pats of butter scattered randomly on top. Mix the sherry and half-and-half. Pour the mixture over the baking dish, and bake for about 30 minutes or until golden.

MAKES 4 SERVINGS

OYSTER SKILLET

One of the most requested recipes of The Old Post Office, Oyster Skillet is entirely dependent on the quality of the oysters. On Edisto in the "R" months, it is unspeakably delicious.

36	small oysters with liquor
1	tablespoon Michel Mix
2	tablespoons melted butter (use Plugra butter)
1	tablespoon freshly squeezed lemon juice

Preheat the broiler. In a 4-inch cast iron skillet put in the oysters, Michel Mix, butter, and lemon juice. Mix gently, and put the skillet under the broiler. Watch for the edges of the oysters to curl and all the oysters are just heated through. Depending on the integrity of the broiler, this should not take more than a few minutes. You can also cut time by heating the skillet before adding the ingredients. Serve with toasted baguettes. The real beauty of this dish is the juice remaining after the oysters are eaten. "Dunk" the bread in the skillet liquor.

MAKES 2 SERVINGS

Variation: "I must say some of the smaller 'pasta purses' or cheese-filled raviolis have gotten better over the years," Philip notes. "They can be very good added to the oyster skillet. Or try about a quarter cup of old-fashioned, cooked egg noodles."

Lowcountry Cooking

The Lowcountry is the southernmost part of South Carolina, a ten-thousand-square-mile triangle of verdant plain bordered by the ocean, the Savannah River, and the hills west of Orangeburg. It is a subtropical region where ocean breezes cool the coast but summer heat waves exceed one hundred degrees. Its swampy woods are home to 'gators, deer, graceful birds, and exotic serpents. Its soil is a prolific source of full-flavored vegetables; its rivers and ponds abound with shad, porgy, catfish, sturgeon, oysters, and herring; and the ocean yields shrimp, crab, and flounder.

The hub of the Lowcountry is Charleston; and while the coastal plain is very much a part of the Deep South, Charlestonians see themselves as a breed apart with a distinguished history and complex multicultural heritage all their own. Their story begins with the Native Americans for whom so many places and landmarks were named (including Edisto, after the Edistow tribe) and includes settlers from the British Isles as well as French Huguenots and slaves transported from West Africa. The Lowcountry pioneers built an economy from enormous plantations of rice, then indigo, then cotton. And their diverse roots became cornerstones of a culture that is a fortuitous mix of erudition and horse sense.

In his definitive book on the subject, *Hoppin' John's Lowcountry Cooking*, John Martin Taylor wrote, "Nowhere in America did the cooking of master and slave combine so gracefully as it did in the Lowcountry kitchen." Taylor points out that in the period between the Revolutionary War and the Civil War, Charleston was the richest city in

America; its well-to-do citizens imported fine wine and rare groceries from around the world, including West Indies spices and exotic fruits from the Caribbean. That provender was abetted by the abundant yield of local gardens and waterways. White and black cooks applied cooking styles they knew from Europe and Africa to transform the copious provisions into a repertoire of dishes as distinct as any regional cuisine in America.

One of the vital elements of Lowcountry cooking is the population of Gullahs, also known as Geechees—descendants of the slaves. The Gullahs' West African heritage, separated from the rest of the South by their concentration on the seaward islands and on remote plantations, gives the cooking of this region an unusual character comparable to Acadian Louisiana. You can learn all about it at a marvelous restaurant named Gullah Cuisine up in Mount Pleasant (home of sweetgrass basket weaving). Here, since 1997, chef Charlotte Jenkins has made a point of serving meals that reflect the culture of those along the Carolina Coast who speak the patois known as Gullah—a variation of English peppered with West African expressions—and whose cooking reflects the same fusion. Ms. Jenkins' menu features "Gullah rice," which can be a meal unto itself or a side dish for such entrees as fried shrimp, grilled flounder, and smothered chicken. It is stunning rice chock-full of shrimp, shreds of chicken, discs of sausage, and nuggets of vegetables. The rice itself is tinted a glistening mahogany color and fairly radiant with peppery flavor. Here is also the place to savor sweet potato fritters and conch fritters, okra gumbo and she-crab soup, hoppin' john and red rice.

Lowcountry cooking includes a great respect for pork, including distinctive barbecue centered around the city of Orangeburg, but seafood is its glory. Crabs, shrimp, and oysters are nowhere better. Frying shellfish is a local passion; but you will also find brilliant raw oysters on the half shell, freshly harvested from beds in nearby creeks and inlets. And there are pillowy crab cakes that are impossibly sweet as well as big slabs of pearly flounder. Meals built around local fish are especially important on the Lowcountry's sea islands, which are defined not only by the ocean to the east but by the streams and marshes that separate them from the mainland. These islands—Edisto in particular—

are also famous for the produce that thrives in their rich soil and sea air. Fruit has been abundant since the earliest Spanish settlers planted peach and loquat trees and pomegranate bushes; fields that once yielded the world's finest cotton now turn out potatoes, onions, corn, greens, and beans.

For us, what is particularly inviting about this distinctive cuisine is that it continues to thrive in restaurants plain and fancy. The Lowcountry is one of those special eating destinations where there always seem to be far more interesting restaurants than anyone has time or appetite to explore. John Martin Taylor laments that many of the true dishes that defined Lowcountry cooking in times past are now virtually impossible to find—except perhaps in a few homes where tradition is hallowed. But in fact, his own writings as a food preservationist as well as a widespread renaissance of interest in American regional cuisine assure that there is plenty of the real thing for visitors to discover. In a fine restaurant such as The Old Post Office, where Philip Bardin consciously practices respect for local food ways, as well as in modest seafood shacks on the barrier islands and street-corner restaurants in Charleston itself, the Lowcountry's vivid character is there to be savored.

MY ANGEL'S CRAB & ASPARAGUS PIE

Due to a lot of bad advertising campaigns and its image of wimpiness, the poor quiche has assumed an undeserved lowly reputation," Philip declares. "This status is ridiculous; 'egg pies' have been around the Lowcountry since well before quiche hit the restaurant scene in the 1970s. They are elegant; and here is my favorite."

1	(8-inch) pie shell
½	pound freshly picked crabmeat
1	cup grated Gruyere or Swiss cheese
¾	cup half-and-half
3	eggs
1	teaspoon salt
1	teaspoon white pepper
1	dozen asparagus spears, blanched and cooled

Preheat the oven to 400°F. Line the bottom of the pie shell with the crabmeat, spreading evenly. Cover this with the grated cheese. Mix the half-and-half, eggs, salt, and pepper well and pour into the shell. With your fingers, delicately mix all the ingredients in the shell, being careful not to tear the pastry. Arrange the asparagus spears in a symmetric design. Bake for 5 minutes, reduce the heat to 350°F, and bake for an additional 25 to 30 minutes or until nice and golden. Always allow to cool before cutting.

MAKES 4 SERVINGS

O.P.O. CRAB CAKES

Folding in the egg whites gives these cakes the buoyancy of a soufflé. Baking, rather than frying, abets their fluffiness.

1	pound jumbo lump crabmeat
1	pound claw crabmeat
1	cup high quality mayonnaise (Hellmann's is a good one)
¼	cup Dijon mustard
1	tablespoon Old Bay Seasoning
	Juice of 1 lemon
1	cup panko (Japanese breadcrumbs)
2	egg whites, stiffly beaten

Preheat the oven to 475°F. Make sure there are no shells in the crabmeat and that the meat is moist but not watery. Gently mix the crabmeats, mayonnaise, mustard, Old Bay, lemon juice, and panko, being careful not to break up the lump crabmeat too much. Fold in the beaten egg whites. Using about a 4-ounce ice cream scoop, scoop out cakes onto an oiled baking sheet. You can make large or small cakes. Bake for 12 to 15 minutes until the cakes are fluffy and golden. Serve with Mousseline Sauce (page 86). This can make as many as 20 cakes depending on your scoop size. Half or quarter the recipe if you do not want that many, but I suggest making and holding a big batch. This mixture holds very well for several days in the refrigerator. If you omit the egg whites, you have a respectable crab salad.

MAKES 4 SERVINGS

STONE CRAB CLAWS & SHRIMP

H ere is my favorite recipe in the book," Philip declares. "Many people do not know that stone crabs are plentiful in Lowcountry creeks. The shrimp take on a magnificent flavor after the claws are boiled."

1	quart (4 cups) court-bouillon (page 88)
8	stone crab claws
2	dozen very fresh, shell-on shrimp with heads removed
	Fresh lemon wedges

Bring the court-bouillon to a boil, and boil the crab claws for 5 minutes and remove. Reduce the court-bouillon an additional 5 minutes. Then boil the shrimp for exactly 1 minute and strain. Serve the shrimp in a big bowl with the crab claws and fresh lemon wedges. A great porch and an ice-cold beer are essential with this.

MAKES 2 SERVINGS

SHRIMP WITH FETA, CAPERS & OUZO

The legendary late Columbia, South Carolina, restaurant, the Elite Epicurean, served a dish similar to this. It resembles some of the Greek seafood preparations you find in the Greek restaurants of Tarpon Springs, Florida.

1	tablespoon butter
12	shrimp, peeled with tails left on
12	small capers, rinsed and dry
1	teaspoon salt
1	teaspoon cayenne
2	teaspoons fresh lemon juice
6	(1-inch) cubes feta cheese
1	tablespoon ouzo (sweet, anise-flavored liqueur)

In a sauté pan over medium-high heat melt the butter, and cook the shrimp quickly with the capers, salt, and cayenne, adding the lemon juice at the end. Do this very quickly—just a few minutes—and be careful not to have the shrimp cooked quite all the way through. Put the shrimp and all the juices in a ceramic, shallow baking dish. Arrange the feta cheese in a symmetric pattern, and put the dish under a hot broiler just for about 1 minute. Remove, add the ouzo, and light it with a match quickly.

MAKES 2 SERVINGS

SHRIMP IN GRAND MARNIER SAUCE

The orange-flavored cognac Grand Marnier was invented in 1880 by Louis Alexandre Marnier-Lapostolle. At the time, bitter oranges from the Caribbean were rarer even than cognac.

1	*tablespoon butter*
1	*tablespoon olive oil*
1	*shallot, finely minced*
24	*shrimp, peeled and deveined with tails left on*
1	*cup thinly sliced mushrooms*
2	*teaspoons salt*
1	*teaspoon cayenne*
¼	*cup Grand Marnier*

Melt the butter and olive oil in a sauté pan on medium heat, and cook to soften the shallot. Turn the heat up to high, and sauté the shrimp and mushrooms quickly until the shrimp are just done. Add the salt and cayenne. Add the Grand Marnier, and if you have a gas stove, tilt the pan just enough to flame. Reduce for less than a minute and serve.

MAKES 4 SERVINGS

FRESH SHRIMP WITH CREAMY PASTA

It is hard to resist any Alfredo-style dish. Here is an easy one to make.

24	*shrimp, peeled*
2	*tablespoons butter*
1	*tablespoon Michel Mix (page 96)*
1	*cup heavy cream*
½	*cup freshly grated, high quality Parmesan cheese*
	Angel hair pasta, about ½ pound
	Salt
	Parsley

Prepare a big pot of boiling salted water for the pasta. In a saucepan melt the butter, add the Michel Mix, and sauté the shrimp until halfway done (just a few minutes). Remove the shrimp from the saucepan and keep warm. Add the heavy cream to the pan and bring to a boil. With a wooden spoon, stir in the Parmesan cheese and reduce the sauce until thick. Put the pasta in the boiling water. (Never add oil to the water, and always use high-quality Italian brands). As soon as the pasta is done al dente, strain. Mix the sauce with the shrimp, check for salt, and pour the sauce over the pasta. Top with chopped parsley.

MAKES 4 SERVINGS

Note: For the particularly skilled cook, an old trick my father taught me eliminated the boiling of the angel hair. He simply put it over the sauce and shrimp as it was cooking and put a lid over it. After 3 minutes or so, the pasta was done; but I have found this technique risky and better with sauce reductions that involve stocks rather than cream.

SHRIMP CREOLE

Philip Bardin's Shrimp Creole is a stew as bright-colored as it is brilliant-flavored. You want the shrimp cooked, but not too long. Do not add them until the sauce is well-simmered.

2	cloves garlic, thinly sliced
2	tablespoons olive oil
1	tablespoon butter
1	teaspoon celery salt
2	teaspoons paprika
1	tablespoon kosher salt
1	tablespoon oregano
1	teaspoon cayenne
1	large onion, thinly sliced
2	stalks celery, thinly sliced
1	green bell pepper, thinly sliced
1	sweet red pepper, thinly sliced
6	ripe tomatoes, blanched and seeded
1	(4-ounce) can tomato paste
1	cup V-8 Juice
1	tablespoon sugar
1	tablespoon sassafras powder (filé)
36	raw shrimp, peeled
	Cooked rice

In a saucepot over medium-high heat, slowly sauté the garlic in the olive oil, and then add the butter and the red pepper, salt, oregano, celery salt, paprika, and cayenne. Turn the heat to high, add the onion, celery, and green pepper, and cook until fairly translucent, about 5 minutes. Add the ripe tomatoes, tomato paste, V-8 juice, and sugar. Simmer slowly for at least 20 minutes. Add the raw shrimp and the sassafras powder to the bubbling sauce. On medium heat the shrimp will cook in the sauce. Do this for about 3 to 5 minutes or until shrimp are cooked to your liking. Serve over rice.

MAKES 4 TO 6 SERVINGS

SHRIMP & GRITS

The *USA Today* once featured a column called the "50 Great Plates of America" back in the year 2000. We were honored to be chosen to represent South Carolina with this shrimp and grits recipe.

48	shrimp, peeled and deveined
	Butter
	Salt
2	cups O.P.O. Grits (page 108)
4	tablespoons Mousseline Sauce (page 86)

Broil or sauté the shrimp in butter and a little salt until the shrimp turn pink, about 5 minutes. Place on a bed of O.P.O. Grits. Top with the Mousseline Sauce to serve. (Any leftover grits can be pressed flat, chilled, and used for grits cakes the next morning.)

MAKES 4 SERVING

Variation: Scallops are certainly not indigenous to the waters around Edisto, but The Old Post Office has been using sweet Well's scallops from Virginia for fifteen years. Just substitute 32 bay scallops for the shrimp. Bake them at 500°F on the lowest rack in the oven for 5 to 7 minutes with just a little butter, salt, and a squeeze of lemon.

RARE GRILLED SEA SCALLOPS

Fresh U-10 scallops are almost always available in fish markets. They can be as large as half a baseball, and they taste best when cooked on a real charcoal grill.

8	*U-10 scallops (about 3 ounces each is perfect)*
	Olive oil
	Kosher salt
¼	*cup chopped fresh thyme leaves (2 teaspoons dried)*
4	*Key limes, cut in half*

Coat the scallops in olive oil and place on the hottest part of a charcoal grill. Sprinkle with kosher salt and fresh thyme. Take the Key lime halves and place one on top of each scallop. Close the top of the grill and leave for about 3 minutes. Then turn the scallops clockwise instead of over, and squeeze the limes over the top of the scallops. Turn the scallops over on the other side briefly, grill for just 1 minute, and serve hot off the grill as is.

MAKES 4 SERVINGS

SEAFOOD CRÊPES

Late Columbia Cuisenaire Gaither Scott created this dish years ago at a private club. You will need to have at least eight crêpes made a little ahead, along with some béchamel sauce or white sauce. Gaither always put a little fennel in his béchamel.

3	tablespoons butter
3	tablespoons all-purpose flour
2	cups half-and-half
2	teaspoons salt
1	teaspoon white pepper
2	teaspoons fennel seed
1	cup cooked shrimp
1	cup cooked scallops
8	crêpes

Melt the butter and whisk in the flour over low to medium heat in a saucepan. Add the half-and-half gradually, and add the salt, white pepper, and fennel. Cook until the sauce is thick. Pour through a strainer to remove the fennel. To this mixture, add the cooked shrimp and scallops and heat through. With a slotted spoon fill the crêpes with the seafood, and roll up and keep warm on a platter in a warm oven. Should make about 8 crêpes. Drizzle the remaining sauce over the top of the crêpes and serve. At the club where I made these, they were often made ahead, chilled, and microwaved. As revolting as this may sound, it works fairly well.

MAKES 4 SERVINGS

"NEEDS HELP" GRILLED TUNA

Fresh yellowfin tuna is abundant on Edisto, but Philip confesses, "I find tuna lacking in flavor. Overcooked, it is a disaster; and most people expect it grilled medium rare, which is not so safe these days. So it is one dish I often mask by using the old fisherman's trick of marinating it in Italian dressing prior to the grill."

4	(4-ounce) tuna steaks
	O.P.O. House Dressing (page 92)
1	cup Mustard Tarragon Sauce (page 87)

In a plastic bag marinate the tuna in the house dressing for about 30 minutes. Drain fairly well or your grill will certainly catch fire. Grill to the desired degree of doneness. Top with the sauce.

MAKES 4 SERVINGS

TUNA FOR SALAD

Someone once wrote that grilled fresh tuna was the worst thing that ever happened to the classic Nicoise salad. Here is a great trick if you are using cooked tuna in a casserole or salad such as the Nicoise.

	Kosher salt
4	*(4-ounce) tuna steaks*
	Olive oil to cover steaks
12	*anchovy fillets*

Salt the tuna liberally and place in a small pot that fits the tuna snugly. Cover with oil and place the anchovy fillets over the top. Cover with a tight fitting lid, and over very low heat and with a watchful eye, let the tuna cook fully, about 12 minutes. Remove from the heat and let stand. This is somewhat tedious and commands undivided attention. Cool to room temperature and refrigerate. Prior to use, drain off the oil and anchovies.

MAKES 4 SERVINGS

SALMON WITH SPINACH MOUSSE & MALTAISE SAUCE

Those times of the year when local fish are not available are opportunities to do something with salmon, even if it is farm salmon (not as tasty as wild Atlantic salmon). Philip refers to this recipe as "a bit too contrived," but nevertheless, it is a customer favorite.

2	cups braised spinach, well drained and salted
4	ounces cream cheese
1	teaspoon lemon
1	teaspoon salt
1	teaspoon cumin
4	(4-ounce) salmon fillets, cut at an angle.
	Salt (or seafood seasoning)
	Maltaise Sauce (variation on page 85)

Preheat the oven to 500°F. Put the spinach, cream cheese, lemon, salt, and cumin in a food processor and blend. Cut the salmon through the center almost to the bottom, making a "pouch." Season the salmon with a little salt or even seafood seasoning. Fill each "pouch" with the spinach mousse, and bake for 7 to 10 minutes. Top with the Maltaise Sauce.

MAKES 4 SERVINGS

Note: For the mousse, using goat cheese instead of cream cheese adds a more robust flavor.

STEAMED BOWL OF MUSSELS

The aroma of mussels steamed in wine and garlic is an epicurean delight. Aside from being delicious, this is a fun dish to make.

1	tablespoon butter
1	tablespoon Michel Mix (page 96)
1	medium ripe tomato, cut into small pieces
24	mussels, scrubbed clean and beards removed
½	cup dry white wine
2	tablespoons heavy cream
2	teaspoons salt
	Freshly chopped parsley
	Lemon

Select a pot that has a tight fitting lid. Melt the butter on high heat, and add the Michel Mix and the tomato. Add the mussels and wine, bring to a boil, and cover. Unless you have a clear lid, you will need to check to see as soon as the mussels open (usually 3 to 5 minutes). I usually pull them all out after the first one pops open, and open the rest manually, a job that is somewhat cumbersome. While arranging the mussels in a bowl, add the cream and salt to the pan juices, and reduce until thick. Garnish with the parsley and lemon.

MAKES 2 TO 4 SERVINGS

EMBRACE OF GROUPER & SOFT-SHELL CRAB

This makes for an excellent presentation and is very tasty.

4	(4-ounce) black grouper fillets
	Melted butter
4	soft-shell crabs
	Milk or egg batter for soaking crabs
	Seafood Breading (page 100)
	Kosher salt
	Mousseline Sauce (page 86)

Preheat the oven to 500°F. Place the grouper fillets in a baking dish and ladle plenty of butter over the top. Cook just until done, about 10 minutes or less, depending on the thickness. Soak the crabs in the milk or egg batter and dust with the breading mix. Deep fry or pan fry the crabs until crispy and golden. Place a crab over the grouper. Lightly salt with kosher salt and top with the Mousseline Sauce. This dish is perfect with the Risotto with Lemon and Goat Cheese (page 106).

MAKES 4 SERVINGS

CAYENNE & HONEY-SIZZLED CATFISH

Philip prefers catfish caught in Lake Marion, but most available catfish are farm-raised in the Mississippi Delta. They have a different flavor, but work fine in this recipe. He advises choosing small fillets.

8	(3-ounce) catfish fillets, soaked in buttermilk and salt (2 tablespoons)
	Seafood Breading (page 100)
	Kosher salt
3	tablespoons freshly squeezed lemon juice
1½	cups hot sauce (Frank's Original)
½	cup honey

Soak the catfish in the salted buttermilk for at least 20 minutes. Have a fryer or a pan of hot oil heated to 350°F. Fry the catfish until golden brown, 4 to 5 minutes, drain, and put in a warm pan (no paper towels). While the fish is really hot, sprinkle it with the kosher salt and lemon juice, and pour the hot sauce and the honey over the fillets. Put the fish on serving plates and pour the remaining sauce over the fish.

MAKES 4 SERVINGS

Note: If you have a rolled steel pan, have it hot first so the lemon juice, sauce, and honey will sizzle. This is excellent topped with our Wasabi Vinaigrette (page 94) if you have some ready in a squeeze bottle. Two fillets per person are plenty.

Variation: The local Baptist preacher, the Rev. Clark McCrary III, is an excellent cook and has developed his own line of sauces. His Tangy Tomato Sauce is outstanding used with sizzled catfish and is a great binder for jambalaya. You will have to order it from him (Parson's Palette at 803-897-3209 or www.theparsonspalate.com). If that is too much trouble, a mix of tomato paste, sugar, cider vinegar, and red pepper flakes with a little liquid smoke comes close. Prepare the exact same recipe as the sizzled catfish, only use McCrary's sauce. Serve with grits and butter beans. It does not get better than this. I think this plate screams for an ice-cold beer, but Clark swears an ice cold Pepsi is the way to go.

MIN'S FRESHWATER FISH WITH CUCUMBERS & DILL

The first time I caught a fish without any help from anyone was a day I went fishing with my glorious Aunt Minnie Lee Blackman," Philip recalls. "It was a large crappie (a silly name, but a fish only a fool would ignore if offered). Min prepared it for me at the Bardin Hotel, and to my horror, I saw her wrap it in foil with cucumbers and some kind of weed-looking thing. I was eight years old."

	Salt and pepper
4	*fillets any freshwater fish like crappie or bass, at least 4 ounces each*
12	*very thin cucumbers, soaked in red wine vinegar and sugar for 10 minutes*
8	*fresh sprigs dill (2 per fish)*

Preheat the oven to 350°F. Salt and pepper the fish fillets, and place 3 cucumber slices and 2 sprigs dill on top of each fillet. Wrap tightly in aluminum foil, and bake for about 15 minutes (unwrap one first to make sure it is done since this all depends on the size). Be sure to remove the foil in front of your guests because the aroma is very pleasant. Remove the sprigs of dill and enjoy.

MAKES 4 SERVINGS

Note: I prefer the skin left on, so the fish will need to be scaled.

WILLIAM'S WELLINGTON

A rich and elegant plate of food named for former Old Post Office sous chef Bill Twaler. "We often discussed specials in the bar after work," Philip recalls. "I suggested a menu item with his name and mentioned a Flounder Wellington that was done at a private club where I once worked at."

4	(4-ounce) dolphin fillets, parbaked until halfway cooked and well seasoned with seafood or Cajun seasoning and chilled
4	tablespoons Shrimp Pâte (page 14)
4	(4-inch) squares of puff pastry or short pastry (frozen will do)
	Shrimp Tomato Cream Sauce (page 82)

Preheat the oven to 500°F. Put 1 tablespoon pâte on each dolphin fillet and wrap carefully in the pastry. Bake until golden brown in a greased baking pan, 7 to 10 minutes. Top with the Tomato Cream Sauce.

MAKES 4 SERVINGS

George & Pink

We'd guess that many people who come to Edisto never know about George & Pink. But if you talk about good food with Philip Bardin for even a short while, you'll find out about it. When we first visited the island, Philip clued us in to the delightful place run by "Miss Pink" Brown and her father. It is a vegetable stand down a long unpaved, tree-shaded road off Highway 174. This is where Philip buys vegetables for the restaurant.

George and Pink Brown keep their stand open every day of the year, year-round. That is because there is no "off-season" when it comes to growing things on Edisto, where the climate is always right for some crop, from spring berries to winter squash. "Edisto has the sweetest soil," Pink explained, reminding us that truck farming became a major local enterprise after the arrival of the boll weevil made growing cotton untenable. It is the extraordinarily fertile soil, as well as growing expertise developed by generations of Edistonians, that has made the island a longstanding source of vegetables for markets miles around. The bins at George & Pink always contain something of interest.

In the winter, you'll find beautiful potatoes, yams, squash, red and green peppers, and cabbage, even flavorful tomatoes. Starting early in the spring, Pink gets in cantaloupes that are ultrasweet, and by summer, melons are at their prime. She is renowned for her ability to quick-sniff a cantaloupe and determine its moment of ripeness. By May the sweet corn starts coming. Pink told us that the fresh-picked corn is so delicious that you don't even want to cook it. Just peel off the husk and gnaw the full-flavored kernels right from the cob.

Even if you aren't in the market for vegetables, George & Pink is an especially charming destination. The drive through a virtual tunnel of live oak trees is a magical one where you are reminded just how different Edisto is from the hurly burly world of the mainland. Once you arrive, you find a dirt-floored hut where the vegetables are sold and where free-ranging chickens scratch and cluck and crow all around. And as you walk from your car, you'll likely see Duke—the world's worst guard dog. Duke is a big, lazy fellow who enjoys snoozing in a large flower planter, oblivious to visitors.

GEORGE & PINK'S "A CHURCH GARDEN"

While browsing around the bins full of beautiful vegetables at George & Pink we noticed a dusty little poster on the wall, about three inches by four inches. It was titled "George & Pink Fresh Vegetables Presents A Church Garden." These words were printed below the headline:

THREE ROWS OF SQUASH
1. Squash Indifference
2. Squash Criticism
3. Squash Gossip

FOUR ROWS OF TURNIPS
1. Turn up for meeting
2. Turn up with a smile
3. Turn up with a Visitor
4. Turn up with your Bible

FIVE ROWS OF LETTUCE
1. Let us love one another
2. Let us welcome strangers
3. Let us be faithful to duty
4. Let us truly worship God
5. Let us give liberally as God has blessed us

WHOLE STEAMED PORGY

Not long ago, a restaurant critic gave us a great review, but chastised me because there were bones in the fish," Philip says. "Many people have forgotten that bone-in fish is far more flavorful; but unfortunately, diners are willing to sacrifice flavor for convenience and ease. When I think of porgy, I think of John Martin Taylor, champion of Lowcountry cooking and a genius in the kitchen. He has prepared porgy—a delicious local little pink fish—for me many times, always whole, of course. It is a simple and lovely dish with outstanding flavor. I tried to serve it several times in the restaurant, but customers sent it back because of—you got it—the bones.

3	cups court-bouillon
4	porgies (usually a little less than a pound each), scaled and cleaned but left whole
	Salt and pepper

In a steamer bring the court-bouillon (you can use fish stock or salted water and wine) to a boil at the bottom, and steam the fish, covered, until a toothpick can be inserted without any resistance or gently investigated with a fork, about 10 minutes. Season with salt and pepper to taste. The fish is actually even better cooked with the scales left on, but past experience tells me this is often asking for harsh words.

MAKES 4 SERVINGS

GRILLED DOLPHIN WITH RED BLISS POTATOES & WATERCRESS

This is an everything-at-once dish for a hot summer day.

2	cups mashed red bliss potatoes or Yukon Gold Recipe (page 111)
4	dolphin fillets, grilled until just done
4	small bunches cleaned, chilled, and crisp watercress
	Soy Ginger Vinaigrette (page 93)

Place mashed potatoes in the center of each of four plates. Place the fish partially on the potatoes and the rest on the empty part of the plate. On the other side, place a bunch of watercress with the stem side held in the potatoes. Dress the entire dish with the Soy Ginger Vinaigrette.

MAKES 4 SERVINGS

FLOUNDER & SHRIMP BAKE

Philip Bardin's definition of a great day: a friend, a cast net with shrimp pulled up, and a big flounder on the end of your fishing pole in a Lowcountry creek.

4	*fresh flounder fillets*
2	*dozen fresh shrimp, peeled, deveined, and cooked*
1	*tablespoon butter, melted*
1	*tablespoon kosher salt*
1	*tablespoon olive oil*
1	*teaspoon lemon juice*
½	*cup white wine*
2	*tablespoons heavy cream*

Preheat the oven to 450°F. Arrange the flounder in a baking dish that has been coated with nonstick cooking spray or food release. Be sure it is big enough to hold all the flounder and border the fish with the shrimp. Over the top of the flounder add the butter, salt, olive oil, lemon juice, and wine. Bake until just done, 7 to 10 minutes. Drain all the liquids into a saucepan, add the cream and the cooked shrimp, and reduce until the cream is infused nicely, just a minute or so. Pour the cream and shrimp mixture over the flounder and serve. Perfect with red rice and greens.

MAKES 4 SERVINGS

A-1 WAHOO

For some strange reason, A-1 Steak Sauce was once regarded as something for hillbillies," Philip observes. "Made with zesty, top-quality ingredients, the sauce got a bad name; but my A-1 Wahoo, which I originally did as a trick, has changed many minds."

4	(4-ounce) Wahoo steaks (or King Mackerel will work)
1	tablespoon Michel Mix (page 96)
¾	cup A-1 Steak Sauce

Put the fish steaks in a plastic, sealable bag with the Michel Mix and sauce, and let them marinate while you are heating a charcoal or gas grill. When the grill is hot, remove the fish from the bag and grill for several minutes on each side. Nothing else needs to be done. For best results, wait and announce your marinade after you get all the compliments.

MAKES 4 SERVINGS

FIRECRACKER FLOUNDER

For my money, the most powerful man in the state of South Carolina is Adjutant General Stan Spears who is in charge of the National Guard. He and his lovely wife, Dot, are regulars, and as sure as his troops are ready, so am I with the biggest freshest piece of flounder I can find. General Spears orders this dish every time he comes in without exception.

2	*cups buttermilk*
2	*tablespoons salt*
4	*(4-ounce) flounder fillets*
	Seafood breading (page 100)

Mix the buttermilk and salt in a baking dish and soak the flounder in the salted buttermilk for at least 20 minutes. Have a fryer or a pan of hot oil heated to 350°F. Dredge the flounder fillets through the breading. Fry the flounder until golden brown, 4 to 5 minutes. Drain and put in a warm pan without paper towels. Top immediately with hot Firecracker Sauce (page 83). This is a very spicy dish and is best served with grits or rice.

MAKES 4 SERVINGS

FLOUNDER MICHEL

A dish from one of the first menus at The Old Post Office, Flounder Michel is good for people on salt and fat-restricted diets.

4	(4-ounce) flounder fillets, skin on
4	tablespoons Michel Mix (page 96)
½	cup dry white wine
	Juice of 1 lemon

Preheat the oven to 500°F. In a sprayed baking dish, lay out the flounder fillets. Massage 1 tablespoon Michel Mix in each of the 4 fillets. Be gentle and take your time. Pour the white wine around the borders so not to disturb the mix. Bake until just done, 7 to 10 minutes. Finish with a squeeze of lemon.

MAKES 4 SERVINGS

DOLPHIN "MISS PINK"

Miss Pink Brown remains one of my most cherished Edisto Island friends," Philip says. "We have known each other since we were in our teens; and her business, George and Pink Fresh Vegetables, is the longest-standing business with the same owner in the same location on Edisto. If everyone was as pleasant, peaceful, and genuine as Pink Brown, the world would be trouble free. This is a dish I made in her honor over twelve years ago."

4	*dolphin or mahi fillets, very fresh, about 5 ounces each*
	Seafood seasoning (Old Bay)
8	*perfectly ripe red tomato slices as thin as possible*
4	*tablespoons butter (use Plugra butter)*
1	*tablespoon Michel Mix (page 96)*
16	*leaves lavender basil (or regular basil)*

Grill the dolphin on a charcoal grill and sprinkle with seasoning. I like to do a butterfly cut so it is not too thick. While the fish is grilling, put the butter and Michel Mix in a pan, and place the basil leaves on flat. Do not get the leaves hot since you want the leaves to remain intact and be barely heated so the color sinks through. The pan can be put near the grill or on a warm spot. After turning the dolphin, place 2 tomato slices on the fish just long enough to soften them. The entire grilling process should take no longer than 7 to 10 minutes. Gently place the lavender leaves over the tomatoes and dolphin, and then lightly finish by spooning the butter over it. This is a tricky dish, but takes on a beautiful pink color that can be quite striking. This makes for a perfect dinner with our Boston Lettuce Salad (page 62).

MAKES 4 SERVINGS

PAN-ROASTED BLUEFISH WITH RED WINE & CAPERS

Due to its large population of hunters, farmers, and fisherman, the Lowcountry has often been considered wine ignorant. Nothing could be further from the truth, as Charlestonians were enjoying great French wines before most of the country was yet to be settled. Thomas Johnson was the sommelier at the old Philippe Million restaurant (at that time the only restaurant in America recommended by Relais & Chateau). Thomas was raised in tiny Park Island just above Edisto. This dish came as a result of a discussion we had about the ridiculousness of people avoiding red wines with fish.

	Salt and pepper
4	*(4-ounce) very fresh bluefish fillets*
	Seafood Breading (page 100)
2	*tablespoons butter*
1	*tablespoon olive oil*
1	*shallot, minced*
12	*capers, rinsed and drained*
½	*cup good red wine (a nice Bordeaux or a fat California Cabernet)*

Salt and pepper the bluefish liberally and dust in the seafood breading. In a large sauté pan over medium-high heat, melt the butter in the olive oil until very hot. Add the fish carefully, and turn after the first side down is well browned, about 4 minutes. At this point add the shallot and capers, and cook on medium-high heat until the bluefish is just done, about another 4 minutes or until you can stick a toothpick through. Remove the fish and add the red wine to the pan with the capers and shallot. This will sizzle and can get messy. Stir quickly with a wooden spoon and just long enough to heat the red wine (if you are using gas it will flame up). Pour over the bluefish. I like to add a little extra kosher salt to the top. Serve with the red wine you cooked with.

MAKES 4 SERVINGS

Note: Bluefish has high oil content and must be cooked the day it is caught. Since it is known not to keep long, chefs often shun it. With a fresh catch, it is absolutely delicious and one of my personal favorites.

· POULTRY, LAMB, VEAL & STEAK ·

Pecan Chicken with Blueberry Sauce

Chicken & Dumplings

Perfect Roasted Chicken

Grilled Chicken Curry

Pork Medallions in Blackjack Sauce

Stuffed Pork Tenderloin

Fussed Over Pork Chop

Kielbasa & Shrimp Rice

Filet Moutarde

Filet with Duck Liver Mousse in Pastry

P.B.'s Ultimate Filet

Pepper & Brandy Rib-Eye Steak

BBQ Tender Tails

Etheredge Skillet

Early Skillet

Flank Steak Drambuie

Lamb Steak with Almond & Mint Sauce

Jacob's Lamb Porterhouse

Braised Lamb Shanks

Simmered Lamb in Pastry

Cracklin' Roast Duck Ltd.

Duck Livers in Champagne Sauce

Pecan Quail with Aunt Min's Gravy

Collard-Stuffed Quail

Rosemary Grilled Rabbit

Whole Fried Rabbit & Grits

Veal Edistonian

Veal Rouladen

PECAN CHICKEN WITH BLUEBERRY SAUCE

I put this on as a special one night just to see if anyone would actually go for it," Philip remembers. "The joke was on me, and it has become one of our most requested recipes for the last fifteen years. Personally, I do not care for it at all; but scores of others do."

4	(6-ounce) chicken breasts
2	to 3 cups buttermilk to cover chicken
2	to 3 tablespoons chicken seasoning
¾	cup Pecan Flour (page 99)
1	cup Blueberry Sauce (page 73)

Heat a skillet with peanut oil to 350°F. Soak the chicken breasts in buttermilk to cover. Season the chicken liberally with the chicken seasoning. (McCormick makes a Montreal Chicken Seasoning that is excellent and even better on steak.) Coat the chicken breasts in the pecan flour, and fry until golden and cooked through, 7 to 10 minutes. While they are hot out of the oil, top with the Blueberry Sauce.

MAKES 4 SERVINGS

CHICKEN & DUMPLINGS

This is the ultimate comfort food. While we do not offer this to customers, I make it in the back for the staff or send it out to those under the weather.

4	cups Chicken Stock (page 90)
1	cup potatoes, peeled and diced
½	cup shelled fresh English peas
1	small carrot, peeled and cubed
1	pound chilled biscuit dough
2	eggs, lightly beaten
1	large chicken, cooked and meat pulled off into bite-size pieces
	Salt
	Black pepper

Bring the stock to a boil, and add the potatoes, peas, and carrots. Let simmer on low heat until the vegetables are tender and then return to a boil. Break the biscuit dough into small pinched pieces, drop into the stock, and they will rise and absorb the liquid to make dumplings. Add more stock if needed. Cook about 5 minutes and stir in the eggs. After 1 minute add the chicken, stirring in gently, and then cover. Turn off the heat and allow mixture to stand for 10 minutes before serving. Add salt and pepper to taste.

MAKES 4 SERVINGS

PERFECT ROASTED CHICKEN

Few things are as satisfying as a freshly roasted chicken, especially if you can find a high quality, free-range bird from a small farm. What Philip refers to as "mass-produced ice chickens" simply do not have the same flavor.

3	tablespoons olive oil
3	tablespoons herbes de Provence
1	tablespoon kosher salt
1	large chicken scrubbed with hot water and salt

Preheat the oven to 500°F. Massage the olive oil, herbs, and salt into the bird. The more time you take, the better the result. Roast the bird for 20 minutes uncovered. Reduce the heat to 350°F and continue roasting for 20 minutes per pound.

MAKES 4 SERVINGS

Note: Instead of the herbes de Provence, you can use our Michel Mix (page 96) and thread fresh sprigs of rosemary under the skin. Small potatoes roasted in the pan drippings make a sinful accompaniment.

GRILLED CHICKEN CURRY

This features the complex flavors of the fruit curry sauce. I realized years ago that my favorite curry dish, which I learned in Jamaica and consisted of goat, was raved on only by me. The replacement of a chicken breast cures the critics.

4	(6-ounce) boneless, skinless chicken breasts
2	to 3 tablespoons chicken seasoning
½	teaspoon cayenne
1	cup Curry Sauce (page 71)

Rub the chicken breasts in the poultry seasoning and a little cayenne, depending on how hot you want this dish to be. Grill the chicken breasts until just done and cover with the heated Curry Sauce.

MAKES 4 SERVINGS

Note: I like to take toothpicks, stick a few sage leaves on the topside of the chicken breasts, and grill with the cover down for additional flavor. Be sure to remove the toothpicks before you turn the chicken breasts over.

PORK MEDALLIONS IN BLACKJACK SAUCE

One of the more prominent listed ingredients in a lot of dishes these days is Jack Daniel's. I have always thought it was fine on its own, but we yielded to pressure and have offered this for years.

1	*pork tenderloin, cleaned and cut into 2-inch medallions (about 10)*
½	*cup molasses*
¼	*cup Jack Daniel's whiskey*
¼	*cup honey*
½	*cup cream*

Marinate the medallions in a mixture of the molasses, whiskey, and honey. After about 10 minutes, strain the marinade into a small saucepot, add the cream, and bring to a boil over high heat. Reduce until thick. This is a quick version of our Blackjack Sauce. Sauté or grill the pork medallions for just a few minutes on each side, or you can bake them at 500°F for about 8 minutes.

MAKES 2 TO 4 SERVINGS

STUFFED PORK TENDERLOIN

This is a heartwarming and satisfying offering. It also reheats well, as reported by my dear friend Amanda Kelsey, in case you want need to take a dish to another location.`

2	pork tenderloins, cleaned
	Cajun seasoning
1	tablespoon olive oil
2	cups Country Ham stuffing (variation on page 107)
1	cup Country Ham Gravy (page 98)

Preheat the oven to 450°F. Rub the tenderloins with the seasoning and sear in a hot pan in the olive oil until well browned, about 5 minutes. Cut the tenderloins in half and make a slit lengthwise across the top just deep enough not to pierce the bottom. This yields 4 tenderloin "roasts." Put ½ cup of the stuffing in each "roast," and bake until the top of the stuffing turns brown, about10 minutes. Top with the Country Ham Gravy.

MAKES 4 SERVINGS

FUSSED OVER PORK CHOP

We are lucky to have large pork porterhouse chops supplied from a small farm and processor. This is "fussed over" because the coating of the seasonings can burn on a grill if not watched properly. A good butcher should be able to supply you with a nice chop. You should insist it includes a good part of tenderloin.

½	cup brown sugar
¼	cup paprika
1	tablespoon white pepper
2	tablespoons Worcestershire sauce
2	tablespoons water
4	(16-ounce) pork porterhouse chops

Mix the brown sugar, paprika, white pepper, Worcestershire sauce, and water in a bowl to make a rub. Massage the rub in to the chops. Let them stand in the refrigerator for at least 8 hours. Prepare a grill to medium hot and grill the chops for 10 minutes on each side. (If your grill has a cover, put the lid down). Check for doneness and serve with Mustard Tarragon Sauce (page 87) and a little of your favorite BBQ sauce.

MAKES 4 SERVINGS

Note: A tablespoon of Accent or MSG does indeed work wonders in the rub. If you are not concerned or a participant in the health debate over this ingredient, by all means add it.

KIELBASA & SHRIMP RICE

Occasionally, we will offer this under a nice piece of fried fish. Store-bought Kielbasa is one of the few premade items in a grocery store I have always found to be very good and irresistible. On its own this makes for an excellent main course.

½	pound Kielbasa, cut into 1-inch rings
1	small onion, halved and sliced
1	bell pepper, halved and sliced
24	peeled and deveined fresh shrimp
1	tablespoon Cajun seasoning
1	tablespoon olive oil
2	cups cooked rice
3	tablespoons Teriyaki Sauce (page 76)

In a large sauté pan heat the olive oil on medium-high heat. Add the Kielbasa and brown, about 3 minutes. Add the onion, pepper, and shrimp and season with the Cajun spice and sauté until the shrimp are just done, about 5 minutes. Add the teriyaki sauce and allow it to coat everything in the pan. Stir in the rice and cook for about 1 minute.

MAKES 4 SERVINGS

FILET MOUTARDE

There is no cut of beef less imaginative and lacking in flavor than a filet mignon," Philip declares. "It is desperately in need of additives and often wrapped in bacon and strong, reduced sauces such as a Béarnaise."

4	(10-ounce) beef tenderloins
1	cup Mustard Tarragon Sauce (page 87)

Grill the center-cut, beef tenderloin filets over a charcoal grill to desired degree of doneness. (Rare is the best.) Top with our Mustard Tarragon Sauce.

MAKES 4 SERVINGS

FILET WITH DUCK LIVER MOUSSE IN PASTRY

This is Philip's answer to Beef Wellington. It is involved, though; he needs a week to prepare for the dish, so customers have to plan ahead for this one.

4	*(4-ounce) filet mignons*
4	*ounces Duck Liver Mousse (page 26)*
4	*(4-inch-square) puff pastries*

In a very hot pan, sear the filets so they have a very crisp outside and are left rare in the middle, just a few minutes each side. Allow to cool and then freeze for 5 minutes.

Preheat the oven to 450°F. Carefully spread 1 ounce Duck Liver Mousse on each filet, and carefully wrap it in the puff pastry. Bake in the oven until the pastry is golden, 7 to 10 minutes. Serve at once.

MAKES 4 SERVINGS

P.B.'S ULTIMATE FILET

My former sous chef Kevin Dobbs and I were slicing rare tenderloin where some goat cheese had accidentally been left on a cutting board," Philip remembers. "We smeared it on the beef, and viola!—a rich and tender beef dish was created."

4	*(10-ounce) beef tenderloins*
8	*ounces French goat cheese, softened*
1	*cup Mousseline Sauce (page 86)*

Grill each beef tenderloin to rare or medium rare, and top with 2 ounces goat cheese. Allow the cheese to get hot or flash it under a broiler. Top with the Mousseline Sauce to serve.

MAKES 4 SERVINGS

PEPPER & BRANDY RIB-EYE STEAK

Life is too short to have anything less than a rib-eye graded USDA choice or higher," Philip believes. "We always use a 14-ounce cut."

2	*(14-ounce) rib-eye steaks*
	Olive oil
	Freshly ground black pepper
	Butter
4	*ounces brandy*
	Salt

Rub the rib-eyes in olive oil and pepper, and sauté in butter until brown and crisp, about 4 minutes on each side. Finish with a shot of good brandy and then salt to taste at the finish.

MAKES 2 SERVINGS

Note: "A contender for the best cheese steak ever was inspired on campus at the University of South Carolina," says Philip. He calls them Carolina Rib-Eyes.

Variation: "Prepare the Pepper and Brandy Rib-Eyes. Top each steak with 2 ounces of our Pimiento Cheese (page 25) and melt under a broiler. Top with a little Mousseline Sauce (page 86)."

BBQ TENDER TAILS

Sometimes you can work a deal with your butcher to get the tails of beef tenderloin at a bargain price.

2	tablespoons balsamic vinegar
2	tablespoons jerk seasoning (not too hot)
1	tablespoon peanut oil
2	tablespoons Worcestershire sauce
1	tablespoon Michel Mix (page 96)
4	(3-ounce) beef tenderloin tails

Combine the vinegar, jerk seasoning, peanut oil, Worcestershire, and Michel Mix in a plastic bag and marinate the beef for at least 1 hour, making sure the meat is evenly coated. Grill or pan fry to desired doneness. Any leftover liquid should be heated, reduced, and poured over the tenderloin tails.

MAKES 4 SERVINGS

ETHEREDGE SKILLET

We love our four-inch iron skillets at The Old Post Office," Philip says. "At one time we had four different skillet main courses. The Etheredge Skillet, inspired by the Depression, is comprised of leftover sausage and grits from breakfast and served later for dinner. One skillet is enough for two, but I prefer it as a single large serving."

1½	cups hot, cooked O.P.O. Grits (page 108)
1	cup cooked and cut onion sausage or Italian rope sausage
½	cup sharp Cheddar cheese

Preheat the oven to 375°F. Using a well-seasoned, 4-inch, cast iron skillet, layer the grits first, then the sausage. Stir ever so slightly and top with the Cheddar cheese. Bake until the cheese is melted, about 10 minutes.

MAKES 2 SERVINGS

EARLY SKILLET

A meal attributed to Judge Doyet A. "Jack" Early of Bamberg, South Carolina, whom Philip calls "a sly and skillful" home cook, Early Skillet uses an ingredient seldom found outside the South and definitely one for which you must have an acquired taste: liver pudding.

4	ounces liver pudding in a casing
1½	cups cooked O.P.O. Grits (page 108)
1	small onion, thinly sliced and sautéed in butter
½	cup Gruyère cheese (grated)

Preheat the oven to 425°F. Cook the liver pudding until just done, about 10 minutes. Allow to cool. Pour the grits into a 4-inch cast iron skillet. Carefully remove the liver pudding from its casing and layer it evenly over the grits. Top with the sautéed onion and the cheese, and bake for 10 minutes. I like to call this dish "Edisto Onion Soup."

MAKES 2 SERVINGS

179

FLANK STEAK DRAMBUIE

Flank steak is usually inexpensive and far more flavorful than many cuts of beef. It is also disappearing from menus where it once had a strong foothold. This version was inspired by many of the unheralded great dishes I have recreated from Scotland and Ireland.

1½	*pounds flank steak*
4	*tablespoons Michel Mix (page 96)*
1	*tablespoon herbes de Provence*
1	*cup Drambuie*
½	*cup red wine*

Rub the flank steak with the Michel Mix and herbs thoroughly, and let stand in the Drambuie and wine for at least 30 minutes. Meanwhile heat a grill. Pat dry the flank steak and grill 5 minutes on each side. While the steak is cooking, reduce the marinade in a saucepan by half. After the steak is cooked, let stand for 5 minutes, and then carve thin slices at an angle. Try to save all the juices on the cutting board, add the juices to the sauce reduction, and reheat the sauce. Salt the slices, arrange on plates, and top with the sauce.

MAKES 4 SERVINGS

Note: If you can find them, veal flanks are wonderful. Skip the Drambuie and simply top with Marsala Sauce.

LAMB STEAK WITH ALMOND & MINT SAUCE

This is a delightful spring dish from The Old Post Office's opening-night menu.

2	(6-ounce) center-cut leg of lamb steaks, bone in
1	cup red wine
2	garlic cloves, crushed
4	sprigs fresh, pungent rosemary
1	tablespoon butter
1	tablespoon olive oil
½	cup slivered almonds
3	tablespoons mint and pepper jelly (preferably homemade)
	Salt and pepper

Marinate the lamb steaks in the red wine, garlic, and rosemary for about 30 minutes. In a large sauté pan melt the butter with the olive oil until very hot. Pan-sear the steaks to your preferred degree of doneness (I like mine done just a few minutes each side). Plate the steaks. Add the almonds to the pan, and toast them, being careful not to let them burn. Remove the pan from the heat, and stir in the jelly, which will melt nicely (you can microwave it first if you would prefer a smoother sauce). Top the steaks with the sauce, and sprinkle salt and pepper lightly to finish.

MAKES 2 SERVINGS

JACOB'S LAMB PORTERHOUSE

Orangeburg native Jacob Dupree is the best cook I know," Philip says. "He is not a professional chef, but rather a salesman for one of the world's largest food companies (Sysco Foods). Despite the hustle and bustle of food sales, at home Jack is a purist with flavors. We did lamb porterhouse together for a special dinner for the Casa Lopostolle Vineyards."

4	(8-ounce) lamb porterhouse steaks
	Salt
	Black pepper
1	tablespoon olive oil
1	tablespoon butter

The beauty of this dish is simplicity, but your lamb must be very fresh and of high quality. Preheat the oven to 400°F. Season the lamb with the salt and black pepper to taste and nothing else. These are too good to ruin with a marinade. Heat the butter and olive oil in a cast iron skillet until very hot. Sear on both sides just a few minutes, and then put the pan with the lamb steaks in the oven and roast for about 10 minutes. Remove and let stand 5 minutes before serving.

MAKES 4 SERVINGS

Note: Like Jack, I prefer this dish done simply. However, a light demi-glace or peppercorn sauce is very appealing to many.

BRAISED LAMB SHANKS

On a cold night, a nice braised lamb shank is a great feast and easy to do. Peter Duffy who runs the Duffy Tavern (only open on St. Patrick's Day) in Charleston taught me this dish.

4	(6-ounce) lamb foreshanks
	Salt and pepper
	All-purpose flour for coating
1	tablespoon butter
1	tablespoon olive oil
2	medium carrots, peeled and cut in 1-inch rings
1	medium onion, thinly sliced
4	sprigs rosemary
2	cups red wine
2	tablespoons sherry vinegar
1	tablespoon cornstarch
1	tablespoon water

Preheat the oven to 375°F. Coat the lamb shanks lightly with salt and pepper and coat with the flour. Sauté the steaks in a hot skillet with the butter and olive oil, turning frequently to brown evenly. Remove to a heavy, deep baking dish. Add the carrots, onion, and rosemary to the pan, and sauté quickly, just 1 or 2 minutes. Then add the red wine and bring to a boil. As soon as it reaches the boiling point, pour the liquid over the shanks and cover tightly in aluminum foil. Bake in the oven for about 50 minutes to 1 hour. Remove from the oven and carefully remove the foil. Check for doneness; you want the shanks tender. Remove the rosemary and discard. Pour all the pan drippings into a saucepan. Mix the cornstarch and water (or make a roux with 1 tablespoon butter and flour) and add to the drippings to make the sauce. Serve one shank per person, making sure each serving gets carrots and onions with the sauce, and serve over a bed of Mashed Yukon Gold Potatoes (page 111).

MAKES 4 SERVINGS

SIMMERED LAMB IN PASTRY

Tender isn't a gentle enough word to describe the velvet-soft character of lamb pulled from the shanks, then cooked with vegetables under a lid of golden-crusted biscuit dough.

4	*(6-ounce) lamb foreshanks*
	Salt and pepper
	All-purpose flour for coating
1	*tablespoon butter*
1	*tablespoon olive oil*
2	*medium carrots, peeled and cut in 1-inch rings*
1	*medium onion, thinly sliced*
1	*cup thinly sliced mushrooms*
4	*sprigs rosemary*
2	*cups red wine*
2	*tablespoons sherry vinegar*
1	*tablespoon cornstarch*
1	*tablespoon water*
1	*(10-count) can biscuit dough, rolled out*

Preheat the oven to 375°F. Coat the lamb shanks lightly with salt and pepper and coat with the flour. Sauté the steaks in a hot skillet with the butter and olive oil, turning frequently to brown evenly. Remove to a heavy, deep baking dish. Add the carrots, onion, mushrooms, and rosemary to the pan, and sauté quickly, just 1 or 2 minutes. Then add the red wine and bring to a boil. As soon as it reaches the boiling point, pour the liquid over the shanks and cover tightly in aluminum foil. Bake in the oven for about 50 minutes to 1 hour. Remove from the oven and carefully remove the foil. Check for doneness; you want the shanks tender. Remove the rosemary and discard. When cooled, pull the meat off of the shanks. Pour all the pan drippings into a saucepan over medium heat and add the pulled lamb meat. Mix together the cornstarch and water and add to the sauce a little at a time to thicken. (You can also use a little roux to thicken the sauce.) Divide into four individual casserole dishes and top with a thin layer of puff pastry or biscuit dough. Reduce the oven to 325°F and bake until the pastry is golden, about 10 minutes.

MAKES 4 SERVINGS

CRACKLIN' ROAST DUCK LTD.

Crisp duckling is often reserved by O.P.O. customers weeks in advance. The restaurant version takes three days to prepare, but for home purposes, this one works fine.

1	*(5-pound) fresh duck*
	Salt
	White pepper
2	*tablespoons dried thyme*
2	*cups orange juice (sour orange juice is best)*
	Blueberry Sauce (page 73) for serving

Preheat the oven to 450°F. Cut the duck in half and remove the backbone. Cut the tips and second joints off the wings. (Save these for a stock, and for goodness sake hang on to the livers for later use.) In a heavy and deep baking dish that has been sprayed with Pam, place the ducks skin side down. Salt and pepper the exposed sides liberally and pour in the orange juice. (You may prefer to use white wine.) Sprinkle the thyme over the top. Seal the baking dish very tightly in aluminum foil, and bake for 15 minutes. Turn the oven down to 350°F and bake for 45 minutes. Remove the foil, being careful not to get a nasty steam burn, and turn the ducks over skin side up. Bake for an additional 15 minutes. Then turn off the oven and let the duck halves remain for another 15 minutes. Pour off all the pan juices, and save them for the many uses described in the accompaniments section of this book. At this point, it is best to chill the ducks in a refrigerator until they are firm again. Reheat in a 500°F oven for 10 to 15 minutes until the skin is crispy and "crackles" when touched with a fork. Serve with Blueberry Sauce underneath.

MAKES 2 SERVINGS

Note: Most of the preparation can be done a day ahead except for the final baking step.

Variation: If you have leftover duck, or want to pull the hot meat off from the method above, add 1 cup hot O.P.O. Grits (page 108) to each cup duck meat, and serve with Country Ham Gravy (page 98). This will win over both those who don't like duck *and* those who don't like grits.

Wildlife

Edisto is an extraordinarily animal-friendly place, and a dreamy destination for eco-tourism. The 1,255-acre Edisto Beach State Park, built by the CCC in the 1930s, is a maritime live-oak forest and salt marsh where visitors come to gather seashells and fossils under tall palmetto trees on the one-and-a-half-mile beach. Nature trails offer walks through the woods and magnificent vistas overlooking the salt marsh; cabins and oceanside tent sites are available to overnight guests. Boat access to tidal waters is permitted year-round, and sport fishing can be enjoyed in tidal creeks and freshwater streams.

For watching birds, as well as indigenous serpents and mammals, there are few locations more productive than the 11,019-acre ACE Basin National Wildlife Refuge, named for the first letters of the Ashepooo, Combahee, and Edisto Rivers that drain the basin. Headquartered in the antebellum home that was once the Grove Plantation, this wonderland is home to countless flocks of birds, both migrating and permanent. These

include bald eagles, peregrine falcons, wood storks, and ruby-throated hummingbirds. Basin wildlife also includes the endangered shortnose sturgeon and loggerhead turtle as well as bobcats, river otters, gray fox, and alligators.

Edistonians are proudest of their loggerhead turtles, as the South Carolina coastline is nesting ground to some 6.5 percent of the world's population of the huge, endangered terrapin. The turtle is, in fact, the official South Carolina state reptile. In 2001 the town of Edisto passed its turtle-friendly lighting law, forbidding any artificial illumination on or near the beach after dusk between May and October, the logic being that lights might confuse newly-hatched turtles and cause them to migrate inland rather than out towards the ocean. In 2002 the Town of Edisto Beach Turtle Project monitored ninety-four nests and counted nearly nine thousand hatchlings.

The easiest place to admire wildlife on Edisto Island is the Serpentarium, just down the road from The Old Post Office. Open from May 1 through Labor Day, this indoor-outdoor environment offers the opportunity to see snakes, gators, and turtles in habitats that approximate nature. The "first true Serpentarium in South Carolina" was opened in 1999 by native Edistonians Teddy and Heyward Clamp, brothers who seem truly to love wildlife and have provided as happy a captivity for their collection as possible: "Alligators and turtles swim and play in large ponds in our outdoor gardens while other reptiles bask in the large, indoor solarium. Also inside, snakes of the world find homes in large displays painted with scenes of their native lands."

DUCK LIVERS IN CHAMPAGNE SAUCE

Swiss born Chef Max Von Salis made this dish with chicken, duck, or goose livers. While he was a chef in Spain, he reportedly made this for the Queen of England. I make this for special occasions and those who are liver aficionados.

½	cup raw, cubed, apple-smoked bacon or sliced strips
2	tablespoons butter
12	duck livers, soaked in buttermilk
	Salt and pepper
	All-purpose flour for coating
1	teaspoon white pepper
1	teaspoon dried thyme
1	cup dry Champagne

Fry the cubed bacon or strips in the butter in a pan or skillet until just browned. Strain the livers, add salt and pepper, coat them in the flour, and add them to the hot pan. Like live ducks, duck livers can be mean, so I suggest a splatter screen to avoid getting popped by grease. When the blood rises to the top of the livers after a few minutes, turn them and cook for 4 to 5 minutes. Add the white pepper, thyme, and Champagne, and reduce until thick, stirring with a wooden spoon. Serve over rice.

MAKES 4 SERVINGS

PECAN QUAIL WITH AUNT MIN'S GRAVY

This is a classic fall dish reminiscent of Minnie Lee Blackman's Sunday suppers at the old Bardin Hotel. Manchester Farms in Dalzell, South Carolina, O.P.O.'s quail supplier, is also a big contributor for charity events.

2	*eggs*
2	*cups milk*
4	*whole boneless quail*
2	*cups peanut oil*
2	*cups Pecan Flour (page 99) for coating*
	Aunt Min's Gravy (page 97)

Mix the eggs and milk and soak the quail for a few minutes. Heat the oil in a large cast iron skillet or a fryer. Coat the quail in the pecan flour, and fry until golden and tender, 12 to 15 minutes. Drain on paper towels and smother in Aunt Min's gravy. Serve with grits and butter beans.

MAKES 4 SERVINGS

Note: As an option true to Minnie's method, you can strain the hot oil, whisk in a tablespoon of flour, add some chicken or duck stock, and finish with a little cream. If you use this method, freshly ground black pepper at the end is essential.

COLLARDS-STUFFED QUAIL

Even for those not fond of greens, this is a hard dish not to like. It is also very easy to prepare and is beautiful when plated.

4	*whole boneless quail*
	Salt and pepper
	Cooked collards, strained
	Flour
1	*tablespoon butter*
	Marsala Sauce (page 72)

Season the quail inside and out with the salt and pepper, and stuff them with the collards (and if you have any pulled meat of any kind—duck, ham hock, etc—by all means include it). You may want to tie the quails' legs together with butcher's twine to keep the stuffing in. Preheat the oven to 425°F. In a sauté pan over medium-high heat melt the butter, and sear the quail quickly on both sides. Put the pan in the oven, and cook the quail through until just done, usually about 12 minutes. (Hint: Heat the collards first and the center will already be warm, and you run less chance of overcooking the bird. Stuffing in this manner, however, is a bit cumbersome.) Cover with the Marsala Sauce.

MAKES 4 SERVINGS

ROSEMARY GRILLED RABBIT

My friend Michael Jordan (not the basketball player) had never finished high school, and at age thirty he became a lawyer. Aside from being a latter-day scholar and a worthy barrister, he is a great cook and outdoorsman. This is a dish we have done many times together.

1	*young dressed rabbit, cut in half with backbone removed*
1	*cup peanut oil*
1	*cup dry white wine*
2	*tablespoons fresh lemon juice*
4	*sprigs rosemary*
1	*tablespoon salt*
	Kosher salt

Marinate the rabbit in a mixture of the olive oil, white wine, lemon juice, rosemary, and salt for 1 hour. Heat a grill—preferably charcoal—to hot and wipe the grill with an oiled cloth to keep the rabbit from sticking. After removing the rabbit from the marinade, place it skin-side down. Shake off the marinade from the rosemary and put a sprig on the top of each half and one under. Place the rabbit directly over the coals or the hottest part of the grill. Cover and cook for 10 minutes. Then turn the rabbit over, and cook uncovered for an additional 10 minutes. This requires careful attention, and if the rabbit starts to burn in spots, move to a less intense heat. Add kosher salt to finish.

MAKES 2 SERVINGS

Note: Some may like a sauce with this, but I like it plain served with rice and hot coleslaw.

WHOLE FRIED RABBIT & GRITS

Due to the recent popularity of whole fried turkeys, lots of people have a big outdoor fryer for the big birds. For a real treat, Philip suggests a whole rabbit. He notes that most turkey-frying folks make the mistake of frying the bird whole, which can make the wings and legs almost inedible by the time the breast is done. He prefers to cook them separately and likes a split rabbit because it cooks evenly.

1	*whole rabbit*
	Buttermilk for soaking
	Seafood Breading (page 100)
	Peanut oil or shortening for frying

Heat a large fryer to 350°F. Cut through the center of a whole young rabbit, and lay it flat, completely spread out but in one piece. Soak the rabbit in the buttermilk to cover and coat it with the breading. Return the rabbit to the buttermilk and coat again. Fry the rabbit until it rises to the top of the oil and is golden, about 15 minutes, and serve on a big platter of O.P.O. grits (page 108). This is a magnificent treat to take to a covered dish dinner party.

MAKES 4 TO 6 SERVINGS

VEAL EDISTONIAN

Veal Edistonian has moved with me to every restaurant at which I have cooked," Philip says. "It originally contained a breading of macadamia nut powder and scallops, two ingredients far away from our region."

4	(2-ounce) veal cutlets, pounded thin
	Buttermilk for soaking
	Pecan Flour (page 99)
1	tablespoon butter
2	teaspoons freshly squeezed lemon juice
¼	cup vermouth
	Salt and pepper
12	shrimp, peeled and freshly broiled
	Mousseline Sauce (page 86)

Soak the cutlets in the buttermilk for about 20 minutes and coat them with the flour. Place in a freezer for 5 minutes. Heat the butter in a sauté pan over medium-high heat, and add the cutlets to the pan. Sauté about 3 minutes on each side and drizzle with the lemon juice. Add the vermouth, which will flame on a gas stove if you skillfully tilt the pan. It is at this point I like to add a little salt and pepper. Top each cutlet with 3 shrimp and the Mousseline Sauce.

MAKES 4 SERVINGS

VEAL ROULADEN

This one is a little tricky, but it has a stunning appearance. For those seeking a dish on the light side, omit any sauces.

2	*(4-ounce) veal cutlets, pounded flat*
8	*spinach leaves, washed*
12	*boiled shrimp*
	Fresh lemon
	Salt and pepper
1	*teaspoon cumin*
	Olive oil
	Marsala Sauce (page 72)

Preheat the oven to 450°F. On the flat veal cutlets, place 4 spinach leaves on each and line with 6 shrimp each. Sprinkle with freshly squeezed lemon juice, and season with the salt, pepper, and cumin. Roll the veal up tightly into two oblong, veal rolls. Cover the rolls with a little olive oil, and cook for about 15 minutes in the oven. Remove from the oven and let stand for 5 minutes. Sauce a plate with the Marsala Sauce. Slice the veal rolls into two-inch rings and arrange on the sauce to serve.

MAKES 2 SERVINGS

·DESSERTS·

Chocolate Mousse
Chocolate Mousse Cake
Chocolate Chip Pound Cake
Charleston Chewy Cake
Coca Cola Cake
Cheesecake
Peach Cobbler
Apples Erickson
Key Lime Pie
Aunt Mae's Lemon Pie
Sweet Potato Bread Pudding

CHOCOLATE MOUSSE

Mary Jane Howell is one of my favorite pen pals," Philip says. "She is the public relations director of the prestigious Dogwood Stable in Aiken, South Carolina. She also loves the flavor of Bailey's Irish Cream, which is the key ingredient in our version of Chocolate Mousse." He suggests serving it with fresh strawberries sprinkled with ground black pepper, or whipped cream and a mint sprig.

6	ounces semisweet chocolate chips
4	tablespoons Bailey's Irish Cream
3	egg yolks
1	cup heavy cream
4	egg whites

In a stainless steel mixing bowl, put the chocolate chips and Irish Cream. Place this over a pot of barely simmering water and melt very slowly, stirring constantly. Rapidly stir in the egg yolks and remove from the heat. Chill the pan quickly over another bowl filled with ice, and refrigerate. Beat the heavy cream in a mixer until thick (many like to add confectioners' sugar and that is an option if it suits your taste). Refrigerate.

In another mixing bowl beat the egg whites until very stiff. After the chocolate bowl is cool (be sure not to overcool or it will turn to a block) but still loose, fold in the cream. Then fold in the egg whites. Cover and refrigerate for at least 4 hours.

MAKES 4 SERVINGS

CHOCOLATE MOUSSE CAKE

This is a silky cake similar to a cheesecake. Philip says that although he lacks the patience of a devoted dessert chef, "From a standpoint of ease, this recipe is tops."

CRUST:

1	cup Oreo cookie crumbs (or cookie of your choice)
¼	cup butter

MOUSSE:

3	(8-ounce) packages cream cheese, softened
3	eggs
1	cup sugar
6	tablespoons Kahlua
8	ounces semisweet chocolate chips, melted
½	cup sour cream
2	tablespoons heavy cream

Preheat the oven to 350°F. For the crust, pulse the cookie crumbs and butter in a food processor. Coat an 8-inch springform pan with nonstick cooking spray, and press the crumb mixture to the bottom, allowing it to come up the sides.

For the mousse, mix the cream cheese, eggs, and sugar until smooth in the food processor. Then add the Kahlua, chocolate chips, sour cream, and heavy cream. Pour this mixture in the cookie-lined springform pan, and bake for about 45 minutes. Turn off the heat, and leave the cake in the oven with the door open slightly for about 1 hour. Refrigerate for at least 1 hour before serving.

MAKES 1 CAKE, 10 SERVINGS

CHOCOLATE CHIP POUND CAKE

Although replaced by other desserts, Chocolate Chip Pound Cake was on the earliest Old Post Office menus; it remains to this day Philip's favorite. He notes that the restaurant uses top-notch Callebaut chocolate from Belgium and emphasizes the importance of high-quality chocolate chips.

2	cups butter, softened
2	cups sugar
9	eggs
1	teaspoon Kahlua
4	cups cake flour
½	teaspoon cream of tartar
½	teaspoon salt
½	cup chocolate chips (high-quality semisweet)

Preheat the oven to 325°F. Cream the butter and sugar in a mixer on low for 3 to 5 minutes. With the mixer running on low speed, add 1 egg at a time and then the Kahlua. While this is mixing, sift the flour, and add the cream of tartar and salt. Add this mixture slowly to the running mixer until smooth. Pour the batter into two, 9 x 5-inch loaf pans sprayed with Pam. Pour the chocolate chips over the top, and slowly stir them into the batter, trying to distribute the chips evenly in the pans. Bake for 1 hour.

MAKES 2 LOAVES, 12 SERVINGS

CHARLESTON CHEWY CAKE

This is a popular, longstanding menu item with a jazzy name. It is really more a large cookie or blonde brownie than a cake.

2	cups light brown sugar
¼	cup butter, melted
2	eggs
½	teaspoon salt
2	cups sifted all-purpose flour
1	cup fresh pecan pieces
1	teaspoon vanilla extract
	Ice cream and caramel sauce for topping, if desired

Preheat the oven to 350°F. Add the brown sugar to the melted butter and mix well. Add in the eggs and salt, mixing very well. Blend in the flour and add the pecans and vanilla. Pour in a 7 x 9-inch baking dish and bake for 25 to 30 minutes. Cut into squares and top with vanilla ice cream and caramel sauce if desired.

MAKES 8 SERVINGS

COCA COLA CAKE

These cakes are very popular and are best if served not long after being baked. Our version was the result of a conspiracy among the restaurant staff while I was away and has since landed on the menu. I must confess I have never made this personally until recently and instead of a Coca Cola I used a Dr. Pepper.

1	cup Coca Cola
½	cup buttermilk
1	cup butter, softened
2	cups sugar
½	cup sour cream
2	eggs, lightly beaten
2	teaspoons vanilla extract
¼	cup cocoa powder
2	cups all purpose flour
1	teaspoon baking soda
2	cups small marshmallows

Preheat the oven to 350°F. Combine the cola and buttermilk in a mixing bowl and set side. In a mixer cream the butter at low speed and gradually add the sugar. When well blended, add the sour cream, eggs, and vanilla. In a separate bowl combine the cocoa, flour, and baking soda. Add this to the butter mixture alternately with the cola mixture. Be sure to begin and finish with the dry mixture. Pour into a standard Bundt cake pan that has been greased and floured. Top with the small marshmallows and bake for 35 minutes. Serve with whipped cream and shaved chocolate.

MAKES 8 SERVINGS

CHEESECAKE

Philip describes Charleston food writer Marion Sullivan as "far and away the best pastry chef in South Carolina for years." He recalls, "Lucky was I—at the mere age of four—to have her briefly as a neighbor. Later, she made desserts for restaurants where I was chef. Her cheesecakes are truly the best. My sous chef makes a mean cheesecake, too, but she will not share the recipe." This is the recipe Philip uses when he makes the cake.

CRUST:

1	cup graham cracker crumbs
2	tablespoons sugar
1	teaspoon ground cinnamon
¼	cup melted butter

FILLING:

4	(8-ounce) packages cream cheese, softened
1	cup sugar
1	pint sour cream
6	egg yolks
3	tablespoons all-purpose flour
2	teaspoons vanilla extract
2	teaspoons lemon juice
6	egg whites

For the crust, put the cracker crumbs, sugar, cinnamon, and butter in the food processor, and pulse until mixed well. Press to line an 8-inch springform pan with the crumb mixture, pushing up the sides several inches. Preheat the oven to 350°F.

For the filling, cream the softened cheese with the sugar and sour cream, and add in the egg yolks one at a time, making sure all is blended very well. Add the flour, vanilla, and lemon. In a large bowl whip the egg whites until very stiff. Fold them gently into the cream cheese mixture, making sure it is not overly folded yet with no visible streaks of egg whites. Pour the filling into the pan and spread evenly. Bake for 1 hour, turn the oven off, and prop the door open for an additional 30 minutes. Remove the cheesecake, let it cool on a wire rack for 1 hour, and then refrigerate.

MAKES 1 CAKE, 10 SERVINGS

PEACH COBBLER

My fabulous kitchen ladies make all kinds of cobblers," Philip exults. An extended peach season means that peach cobbler is on the menu from early spring to fall.

7	*large, ripe peaches, skinned, pitted, and thinly sliced*
1	*cup brown sugar*
2	*tablespoons ground cinnamon*
3	*tablespoons butter*
1	*tablespoon lemon juice*
1	*cup all-purpose flour, sifted*
1	*teaspoon baking powder*
¼	*teaspoon baking soda*
½	*teaspoon salt*
3	*tablespoons shortening*
¾	*cup buttermilk*
	Peach or vanilla ice cream, optional

Preheat the oven to 425°F. Coat a 7 x 9-inch, ovenproof baking dish with nonstick spray. Mix the peaches with the brown sugar and cinnamon, and spread over the bottom of the baking dish. Dot with dabs of the butter. Sprinkle the lemon juice over the top and bake for 25 minutes.

In a mixing bowl, sift the flour, baking powder, baking soda, and salt. Add the shortening in pieces, and rub this mixture in the palms of your hands to make "beads." Slowly add the buttermilk. After the peaches are baked, dollop the flour/buttermilk mixture on top of the peaches, and bake for another 20 minutes or until the topping has browned. Serve with peach or vanilla ice cream.

MAKES 6 SERVINGS

APPLES ERICKSON

Philip named Apples Erickson for his friends Jane and Greg Erickson, who live near the great apple orchards in Hendersonville, North Carolina. When they come to town, he makes this dish in their honor; and he suggests serving it with strong Irish coffee.

4	*Fuji apples, peeled, cored, and thinly sliced*
4	*tablespoons butter*
½	*cup brown sugar*
1	*tablespoon ground cinnamon*
1	*teaspoon lemon juice*
1	*tablespoon honey*
4	*(4-inch) puff pastry squares*

Sauté the Fuji apples in the butter, and add the brown sugar, cinnamon, lemon juice, and honey. Reduce until thick, and cool to room temperature. Preheat the oven to 350°F while the apple mixture is cooling. Spoon the apple mixture into the puff pastry squares, and shape any way you like. Bake until browned, about 15 to 20 minutes.

MAKES 4 SERVINGS

KEY LIME PIE

The O.P.O. makes Key Lime Pie in individual ceramic baking dishes lined with graham cracker crumbs or ginger snap crumbs. This recipe makes a single 9-inch pie.

CRUST:

1¼   cups graham cracker crumbs

2   tablespoons sugar

4   tablespoons butter, melted

FILLING:

3   large egg yolks

1   (14-ounce) can sweetened condensed milk

½   cup fresh Key lime juice (or Joe and Nellie's Key Lime Juice)

       Whipped cream or cream cheese topping, optional

Preheat the oven to 350°F. Mix the crumbs, sugar, and butter in a food processor, and line a 9-inch glass pie plate. Bake for 10 minutes, remove, and let cool. In a mixing bowl start with the egg yolks and slowly whisk in the condensed milk, then the lime juice. Pour the mixture into the piecrust and bake for 15 minutes. Remove, cool, and refrigerate. Serve with whipped cream if desired or with a cream cheese topping.

MAKES 8 SERVINGS

AUNT MAE'S LEMON PIE

My late Aunt Min has always been trumpeted as the great chef of our family," Philip says, adding, "One little-known secret was she didn't care to make desserts. Her younger sister, my Aunt Jessie Mae, was a whiz at pie making. She also loved cornflakes: potatoes baked in rolled cornflakes, cornflakes plain, cornflakes with sweet milk and pecans, etc. Her lemon pie has a cornflake crust."

CRUST:

4	cups cornflakes
⅔	cup melted butter
¼	cup sugar

FILLING:

3	egg yolks
5	tablespoons sugar
2	tablespoons water
3	tablespoons lemon juice
3	egg whites
2	tablespoons confectioners' sugar

Preheat the oven to 350°F. For the crust, blend the cornflakes, butter, and sugar in the food processor, and press in a 9-inch glass pie dish. Bake for about 10 minutes. Set out to cool.

For the filling put the yolks in a mixing bowl first, and then add the sugar, water, and lemon juice. Heat in a double boiler until thick. Cool.

In a separate bowl whip the egg whites and confectioners' sugar until stiff peaks form. Gently fold the egg whites into the lemon mixture and fill the piecrust. Bake for 10 to 12 minutes until nicely browned.

MAKES 8 SERVINGS

SWEET POTATO BREAD PUDDING

Bread pudding is always served at fundraisers for the local churches. Philip especially likes it enriched by sweet potatoes, and recommends topping it with whipped cream or Mousseline Sauce (page 86) spiked with bourbon.

12	(1-inch-thick) slices day-old O.P.O. Bread (page 35) or French bread
½	cup butter, softened
4	eggs
2	cups sugar
3	cups half-and-half
1	cup mashed sweet potatoes
2	tablespoons vanilla extract
2	tablespoons brown sugar

Preheat the oven to 350°F. In a glass baking dish sprayed with Pam, line the bread, which should be spread on one side with the softened butter. Place the butter side up. Beat the eggs and sugar until smooth, and add the half-and-half, sweet potatoes, and vanilla. Make sure this is blended very well. Pour the mixture gently in the baking dish and sprinkle the brown sugar on top. Place this baking dish in a larger one and surround it with hot water. Bake for about 40 minutes and then remove from the oven. If the pudding seems loose, it will firm as it cools.

MAKES 8 SERVINGS

INDEX